"Praise the Great Mother for the birth o[...] honesty, beauty, and labor of its autho[...] This book is for all humans who long to sit in the lap of the Holy One and to be nurtured in love and story. Blessed are the women who went before us and who walk with us even now. And blessed is this beautiful creation."

— Rev. Beth A. Richardson, writer, artist, storyteller, and liturgy nerd; Dean Emeritus of The Upper Room Chapel

"Claire McKeever-Burgett has captured the process of midrash in her book and skillfully relates her *midrashic* accounts to the experiences women have had throughout time. She brings to life women in the Christian Scriptures, some named there and others nameless until McKeever-Burgett gives them names and identities. By including her own experience throughout the work, she makes women's stories real as she teaches truth."

— Rabbi Emeritus David Horowitz, Temple Israel Akron, Ohio and Past President, PFLAG NATIONAL

"In *Blessed Are the Women*, Claire McKeever-Burgett lifts up the deep well of women from which we come, and through these women, she offers us audacious vulnerability, expansive liberation, powerful witness, and creative contemplative connection so that we can more fully be healed as we remember–love holds us still."

— Rev. Molly Brummett Wudel, Co-Pastor of Emmaus Way, Durham, North Carolina

"*Blessed Are the Women* is not a story only for women. It's a story for all of us who yearn to embrace the fullness of God's goodness within us and to live and love with the fullness of our enfleshed selves. *Blessed Are the Women*/Claire is a trinity of gentle wisdom, tender mercy, and inexplicable beauty that I will be sharing with colleagues, friends, and parishioners. To know Claire and her work is to know what wisdom, tenderness, brilliance, and grace look like in human flesh."

— The Rev. Maria A. Kane, Ph.D., Rector, St. Paul's Episcopal Church, Waldorf, Maryland

"*Blessed Are the Women* gives voice to the actual daily lives of biblical women. Each woman is visited in her own world, and speaks words of healing and wholeness into our world. These words are given theological depth through original music and liturgy. The music is beautiful (and singable!), the liturgical resources theologically elegant, and the suggestions for action and ethical witness at the end of each chapter open the reader's eyes to new possibilities for changing the world in which we live. I strongly recommend this book for preachers, liturgists, teachers, and small group leaders."

— John S. McClure, Charles G. Finney Emeritus Professor of Preaching and Worship Vanderbilt Divinity School

"This extraordinary book integrates the stories of biblical women, with profound contemporary experiences of women's bodies and sexuality, in ways that are stunning, healing, invitational, and prophetic. The recommended reading, viewing and listening resources and the reflection guide make it accessible and ready to use for individuals or small groups. I can't wait to introduce *Blessed Are the Women* to others, and to use it as a resource for healing retreats and groups for women."

— Elaine A. Heath, Ph.D., Author of *Healing the Wounds of Sexual Abuse: Reading the Bible with Survivors*, and co-author of *Trauma Informed Evangelism: Cultivating Communities of Wounded Healers*

"*Blessed are the Women* is a liberating guidebook for a deeper and wider relationship with God through scripture. Rooted in the author's lived experience, it opens needed space for so many of our stories. The words within its pages show us what it can look like for women to take up space in the story of God."

— Rev. Molly Vetter, Senior Pastor, Westwood United Methodist Church in Los Angeles

"*Blessed Are the Women* invites us to meet and remember Jesus through the lives of women coping with oppressive social and religious realities. Just as our faith journey relies on creative imagination, so does our ability to engage the depths of their stories. They are named. They have traumatic histories. They are strong and courageous. They have much to teach us. This creative rendering of their stories guides our Christian discipleship."

— Luther E. Smith, Jr., Professor Emeritus of Church and Community, Candler School of Theology, Emory University

"Savor this book! *Blessed are the Women* is a tender gift for hungry souls and neglected bodies longing to find gospel companions bearing honest witness to the wonder and frailty of life. Claire's determination to unapologetically proclaim all the news — good, conflicted, life-giving, and incomplete — she's heard from the mothers of the Jesus story and wise women she's met along her own journey will inspire and challenge you."

— Rev. Amos J. Disasa, Senior Pastor, First Presbyterian Church of Dallas

"Claire McKeever-Burgett takes women seriously. Because of that, this book feels both wizened and somehow brand new; ambitious yet matter-of-fact. *Blessed are the Women* was a delightful read."

— Shannon K. Evans, author of *The Mystics Would Like a Word* and *Feminist Prayers for My Daughter*

"For those who long for imagination, long for women's voices to not simply be included but to be celebrated and centered in their faith practice, Claire has written this for you. She has written it for us. Blessed are the women, indeed."

— Jenny Booth Potter, author of *Doing Nothing is No Longer an Option: One Woman's Journey Into Everyday Antiracism*

"This book is premised on the notion that we can expect to hear God's Word anew when we show up to Scripture. Claire is helpfully pointing back to a range of stories (women's stories!) through which we can discover ourselves (and God) again and again. The associated prayers, liturgies, and music enable us to move past a static reading of these narratives and to start living into them, as these women's experiences have the potential to reorient and characterize our lives today. In that sense, it is a gift."

— The Rev. Zachary Thomas Settle, PhD; Editor-in-Chief, *The Other Journal*

"*Blessed Are the Women* is appropriately named, but don't let the title confuse you. This is a book that men need to read also. Given the patriarchal history of American Christianity, we men need to understand how we have been complicit in harming women and how we can be transformed by listening to their wisdom and following their lead. As McKeever-Burgett writes, "Without women we don't have Jesus. We don't have Christianity. We don't have any of it." Christian men would do well to sit with the truth of that statement and reading the stories within this book could enable that truth to sink deep into their souls."

— Rev. Dr. Christopher Carter, Associate Professor of Theology at Methodist Theological School in Ohio, and Lead Pastor of The Loft at Westwood United Methodist Church in Los Angeles

"McKeever-Burgett holds a profoundly incarnational theology, integrating spiritual reflection with practical embodiment. Hers is an original voice, forged in the crucible of her own pain, fear, and grief, tempered by courageous self-examination, intuitive vision, and poetic joy. *Blessed Are the Women* is holistic, designed to foster communities who read, reflect, worship, and share stories together, empowering one another for the sake of healing, freedom, and justice. These pages contain a forceful rebuke of patriarchy and an open invitation to move toward sacred, life-giving wholeness for all."

— Marjorie J. Thompson, author of *Family: The Forming Center* and *Soul Feast: An Invitation to the Christian Spiritual Life*

Benediction by Becca Stevens, Founder of Thistle Farms
CLAIRE K. M^CKEEVER-BURGETT

Blessed Are the Women

Naming and Reclaiming
Women's Stories from the Gospels

chalice
PRESS

Print: 9780827203341

EPUB: 9780827203358

EPDF: 9780827203365

ChalicePress.com

Printed in the United States of America

Wade and Liv,

This book is for you and because of you.

*Your wisdom leads me to deeper healing
and bigger love every moment of every day.*

I love you with my whole heart. Forever and ever. Amen.

Your Mama

* * *

*Mom (Susan Kay Livingston McKeever) and
Dad (Russell Dean McKeever),*

This book is also for you and because of you.

*Thank you for being my first home.
Thank you for showing me what love is.*

Thank you for giving me my life and my name.

I am forever grateful for you and forever anchored by you.

Your daughter, Claire

CONTENTS

For the purposes of this book, I understand "women" as those who stand their sacred ground amid all oppression, find their voices, and use them. Women bring forth life and fight like hell to make that life worth living. Women lead from the margins of society and from the deep center of their beings. Women sit in sacred circles to process, listen, and dance, healing the world one open and honest question, one deep belly laugh, one peaceful melody, and one true, heartfelt story at a time.

* * *

Some of the women's stories in this book, including my own, contain accounts of sexual assault, harassment, mental illness, stalking, cyberbullying, issues of fertility/infertility, and traumatic birth. I give warnings at the beginning of the chapters that contain sensitive content, and I implore you to skip these chapters if reading these narratives might reactivate your own trauma.

* * *

Let your heart lead you into these stories. Let your kindness and generosity overtake any need for certainty. Let your desire for a different way of living and being in the world guide you toward new truth and a bigger love. Let these stories be at the center of your life. Talk about them over lunch, at the dinner table, before bed. Imagine the stories you wish to hear and write them down. Conjure the stories of your own life, and tell them to your children, your sisters, your friends. Just as each of the women in this book have a story to tell, a vision to birth, a song to sing, a sermon to preach—stories, visions, songs, and sermons we've been waiting centuries to hear—so, too, do you. Tell them. Birth them. Sing them. Preach them. We're here. We're listening.

Alleluia! Amen.

I walked to the center of the sixty-five-year-old chapel, cold morning light piercing the windows. I stood dead center without a pulpit blocking me, adorned in a clerical robe and a purple-and-gold stole, which signified it was the season of Lent. A flimsy black music stand held my printed sermon, but my body held the actual sermon. She was ready to preach.

I want Jesus to walk with me

The opening line of the African American spiritual rang throughout the pews, bounced off the tile floors, and soaked into the wooden carvings as I sang.

I want Jesus to walk with me

It felt like a cry, a plea. My most haunting poem. My most honest prayer.

All along life's pilgrim journey, Lord, I want Jesus to walk with me

It was quiet, a collective congregational holding of our breath. What would come next?

I exhaled and began to speak as Eve.

* * *

In March 2018, the dean of The Upper Room Chapel asked me to preach a Lenten sermon at the midweek service. I was currently on The Upper Room staff, working with The Academy for Spiritual Formation in the realm of contemplative spirituality. Having enjoyed pastoring a church prior to my work at The Upper Room, I was eager to accept invitations not only to preach but also to craft liturgy and worship experiences for the community.

I was beginning to understand that my gifts as a writer and communicator weren't merely tools that *helped* me to be pastoral; they were me *being* a pastor. I was beginning to see that a church building, pews, and a pulpit were not necessary for me to embody my pastoral calling to love the world and the people within it. I was awakening to the possibility that I could be most fully me and most authentically pastoral outside traditional church walls.

Moreover, for several months my husband and I had been trying to get pregnant with our second child with no success. I'd awakened that March morning to blood between my legs, and I'd cried in the hot shower before getting ready for the chapel service. As citizens of the United States, we were also two years into the tenure of an American president who frequently reduced women to their body parts as if those body parts were an insult and not the most powerful things on earth.

So later that morning as I stood before the congregation, steady and sure, bleeding and not dying (though my heart felt like it might), I thought, *I'm a miracle. All of us women are.*

It was a season of holding my breath while trying to breathe. Of dressing my child in a shirt that read "Boys will be good humans," as if that shirt were the most fervent prayer I'd ever prayed. Of kneeling at the family altar every twenty-eight to thirty days when I could feel the cramps and knew the blood was coming—not a baby. Of praying through cries and groans too deep for words. Of lighting candles and collecting stones and showing our son icons of Mary, Saint Clare, and Julian of Norwich so he could see (and not only hear of) the women who had formed and were forming me and us all. It was a season of learning to trust what I did not know in order that I might learn to trust what I did.

In this sermon, I'd been instructed to give a nod to Women's History Month. But I'd long considered Women's History Month to be constrained—like how I thought of Black History Month and Native American Heritage Month and all of the other months that relegate certain groups to thirty days instead of acknowledging them as central to the whole year. I wondered, *Is not all of history Black, Native American, and full of women? As if this country would have any of it—this land, these people—without us?*

With these personal and political aggressions swirling, I opened my laptop to search the week's lectionary scripture passages in preparation for the midweek chapel service. And there she was: the woman whose name I did not yet know; the woman who is saved through her love.

As I read Luke 7:36–50,[1] I heard her story as if for the first time—the story beyond the story on the page, the story that told me her name and her circumstances, her longings and her loves, her redemptions and her devastations. And I heard her name: Eve.

Eve first found her way into my heart, then onto the page. Once her presence was rooted within me, I preached her from my sacred and bleeding body that cold Wednesday in March with a congregation of people who quenched themselves with Eve's story. I could feel myself drinking the water with them. With every word and turn of phrase, I stood more confidently on my own two feet. My heartbeat slowed, and I saw Julian, Mary, Clare, and my grandmothers, smiling from the balcony. For us all, drinking that narrative water was a baptism into a new way of being together, and we floated in those waters like we were fish, finally set free.

All told, I wrote Eve's story in a couple of hours. She poured out of me like water from a fountain. She felt natural, real. As I often do when I preach, I gave her a song to sing, "I Want Jesus to Walk with Me." It served as the refrain holding the narrative together.

Singing the African American spiritual was a way to honor not only her but all those whose names have been forgotten, whose stories have been erased, whose truths have been ignored.

I felt powerful that day, not in a "lording over" kind of way but in a "come let me show you something different" kind of way that gives you a glimpse of what it is to be fully you, unafraid to be known and seen.

Discovering and preaching Eve's story saved me that day. She gave me purpose and passion. She showed me that I could stand on my own two feet even amidst overwhelming sorrow. She reminded

---

[1] A woman visits Jesus as he dines in the home of a Pharisee. She anoints Jesus with perfumed oil and her tears. The Pharisee, Simon, is indignant at her presence and that Jesus is allowing her interaction. Jesus uses Simon's indignance as an opportunity to teach about love and forgiveness, revealing that the woman's love and gratitude are what save her.

me that the good news is always for the broken-hearted. She showed me that all any of us really want is to hear a melody, be drawn into a narrative, and find ourselves there, walking along the dusty road, with Jesus.

I walked back to my office after preaching and wrote on a piece of paper: *I will tell women's stories (and my own) for the rest of my life.*

Preaching Eve's story that day was different from my previous sermons in that I'd never preached as if I were the woman in the text. Prior sermons seemed to dance around the truth instead of speaking it directly. Channeling Eve's story enabled me to share parts of my own story and not feel alone in sharing them. I became Eve, and Eve became me; our connectedness and power were undeniable and palpable. Though I was terrified, I was also delighted; though I was scared, I still named Eve and told her story.

Offering sermons since March 2018 has come in many different forms as my work and witness in the world have evolved. I've also connected through blog pieces, Instagram posts, newsletters, all-staff emails, podcast conversations, letters to my children, birthing babies, and by sharing reminders of love and solidarity in leadership meetings and gifting monthly gifts to organizations that foster justice, love, and mercy. The connecting thread through all of their many and varied forms is the women. They're everywhere.

We need not look far to find them. Women are there in the spaces between the words, in the pause between stanzas, in the barns and back alleys, in the dust and the water. They're at the cross. They're in the next room. They're the mothers weeping and the daughters rejoicing, the patrons supporting and the sisters advocating. They're the ones giving birth, the ones longing to give birth, the ones praying in places in which they're told only men can pray.

Without women, we don't have Jesus. We don't have Christianity. We don't have any of it. Jesus, our Deliverer, can only deliver us because he was first delivered by a woman named Mary.

So within these pages are the stories of women who tell the good news. Some of their names we've known forever. Others have always had names; we just didn't know them. I've named the latter, and each time that naming has felt like a prayer I've longed to speak for years.

These are the stories that I want my children to hear during Advent and on Christmas Eve. On any other ordinary day, I hope they might stumble upon the grace of a liturgy that lends itself to love.

These are the stories that I've wanted to hear on Sunday mornings my entire life. They are the stories I kept waiting for someone else to tell until I finally realized they weren't anyone else's but my own, and ours.

These stories are for all who dare to follow God the Deliverer, the One Who Gives Birth, the One who reminds us, again and again, that we can give birth too.

These stories are gospel.

Part One

[Content Warning: Stalking, Emotional Abuse, Cyber Bullying]

In the beginning, there I was—bright-eyed and hungry, screaming for my mother's breast, longing for her skin. Born via cesarean section, it took a few hours in 1982 to get me to my mother after I was born. However, once we found our way back to each other, I never wanted to leave. She was my first home, after all, and while I do not consciously remember the smell of her skin or the feel of her face, my body remembers her body's blessings. They were sacred and therefore eternal.

My parents named me Claire after my maternal grandmother, Clara, meaning "clear and bright." The youngest daughter of the youngest daughter, the only granddaughter on my father's side, I was born, as we all are, into a particular set of ideas and expectations for what girls and women are meant to be.

Of course, these ideas and expectations are rarely stated. Instead, they hang in the air like oxygen. They are absorbed into the bone and marrow. In fact, scientists tell us they already exist in our DNA. There is such a thing as generational trauma, what I think of as residue from the downpour of expectations and ideas not set *by* women *for* women but by the overarching culture, the men who hoped to keep those women tame, domesticated, subservient. I also believe there is such a thing as generational joy, that our bones and blood know what it is to dance and sing, free from expectation and fear, guided only by our collective hearts' wisdom and love. How else do we explain our survival? For a woman cannot live on sorrow alone.

Geography is significant when telling our stories (there's a reason Jesus frequently talks about fig trees and grapevines—ancient Israel was teeming with them); therefore, it matters that I was born in Abilene, Texas. That city is known as the gateway to the West, its horizon dotted with wily mesquite trees and rough plateaus. In Abilene, sky billows out across the dry plains as far as the eye can see. The land and region of Abilene was originally inhabited by the Comanche people, and it's not lost on me that my formation, due in large part to the West Texas landscapes of my youth, was made possible by the conquest of this land from its original inhabitants. My homelands, then, are not mine, though they are part of me. Yet another opportunity to hold two truths at once, to practice nuance, and to continue the work toward reconciliation and repair with the land, its people, and God.

Juxtaposed with those wide-open plains were the constraints of being raised Southern Baptist in which I was shaped in the Christian faith. As a young girl growing up within this entrenched patriarchal religious system, I was told that if I wanted to work in the church, I could be a missionary, a pastor's wife, or a children's minister. The church allowed women to pray publicly, share their testimonies, and sing, but it never considered these offerings to be sermons. No, the sermon was always given by men, who typically delivered it in a pontificating manner, and it was always too long.

I heard sermons of fire and brimstone, of hell and its horrors. The message always circled back to one theme: if we lived a certain way, avoiding certain people and temptations, we could elude eternal damnation. I heard sermons about love too. Messages of love were sometimes a little harder to discern, but they were there, reminding me that life is a mixed bag, and we will be the better for living the contrasts.

Into this mixed bag I was born. In my family of origin, I have an older brother, a mother, and a father. We love each other eternally. Never have I doubted their love for me. Though seeking their approval and their admiration has been a lifelong quest, I've always known that I am loved simply for being me. Now that I'm a parent myself, I see how intricately intertwined nature and nurture really are; it takes a host of both DNA and life experience to make a person a person, a life a life. Who is to say whether I was drawn to pastoral and spiritual leadership because I was born with gifts for it, or because such leadership was off limits to me being raised Southern Baptist? Perhaps it was both.

As a little girl, when my friends and I played church, I was always the choir director, telling the choir members (my friends) what to do. *Sit here. Sing this. Play in this key. Find this melody. Sway to this rhythm.* My family of origin both celebrated my leadership abilities and felt intimidated by them. My parents encouraged my questions and my voice, yet they didn't fully know what to do with some of the things I would say or challenge. As a parent, I now understand how this mix of celebration and intimidation feels. We do the best with what we know in the moment, trusting God to handle the rest.

It is this entrusting me to God that is perhaps the greatest gift my parents gave me. Whether they ever articulated it or not, especially as I grew older, I could sense their desire to let me be as God would have me be. It wasn't always easy, but they tried and are still trying to release the bone of their bone and the flesh of their flesh to the God of the universe. As the one being released and entrusted, I felt and feel both terrified and delighted all at once. To have parents who say I am not only their daughter but also their pastor imitates Mary and Elizabeth, who each understood from the beginning that while their child is from them and of them, the child is also completely *other* and called to *something beyond.*

Stepping into the "something beyond" has been a two-steps-forward, one-step-back dance since I was eighteen. It was then that I first left home for college in Nashville, Tennessee, a fourteen-hour drive from my parents, my hometown, my wide-open skies, and my wily mesquite-tree-dotted plains. I moved back to Texas after one year in Nashville, though, feeling completely lost and alone. Every time I drove from Texas to Tennessee, I felt as if I were driving to an island with only one way in and one way out. It's funny to think of this now, given that I've lived in Nashville for close to a decade, making this not only *my* home, but *ours* with my family of four. But as a young woman who grew up with a voice and a vision and nowhere to express that voice and vision fully, it took some years to find the best places for those to rest and grow.

During my freshman year of college at Belmont University in Nashville, my teachers introduced me to Dorothy Day, Dietrich Bonhoeffer, and Oscar Romero, three saints who, in turn, introduced me to a radical way of living and being in the world that stood alongside the poor, marginalized, and forgotten. These saints required not a right way to live, but a loving way. They asked questions of God and their faith and invited me into a progressive orientation of living and being in the world that constantly questioned the status quo, asking, "To whom are we not paying attention? Whose voices do we need to hear that we are not hearing?" The way they lived changed the way I lived, or at least the way I wanted to live.

While I was reading their stories and being transformed by them, I was also desperate to be loved, which unfortunately led me into an emotionally abusive relationship for the next two years. Talk about a mixed bag! I was drawn to liberation and love, yet I was trapped in a culture that fostered toxic masculinity and relational abuse, a culture that offered no road map for how to navigate men who, from the beginning, were told they could do what they wanted with whomever they wanted. No wonder I felt lost, alone, broken, and unkempt—all things I was not supposed to be. I, Claire, was supposed to be whole and together. Of course, those of us who have fallen apart know the gift of such falling, the grace of such breaking. We also know that it's laughable for any of us to think we're not a second away from collapsing at any moment, and knowing this fragility, this vulnerability, this humanness is what keeps us close to ourselves, to God, and to others.

Though I moved back to Texas to finish my college career at Baylor University, only three hours from my childhood home, I soon learned that my problems didn't evaporate by changing locations. Indeed, in some ways they multiplied. While academically I found a niche in the English department at Baylor and loved it, socially, I remained confused.

I joined a sorority in which I felt a misfit. I tried out for a choir but was not offered a place in it. I fell in love with my teacher's assistant, who thought me smart and cute but did not share my affections. My ex terrorized me, sometimes calling fifty times a night (thankfully, I learned to put my phone on silent). When he got no response from me, he hacked into my email and sent humiliating messages to my parents about our sexual relationship, shattering their image of their daughter. All of this took place long before the term *cyberstalking* existed, long before colleges woke up to sexual assault and abuse happening on their campuses and among their students, long before survivors' stories were more mainstream. My reality left me in deep shame, unsure of where to go or to whom I could safely talk.

Yet every night as I struggled to sleep, I opened my Bible to the Book of Psalms. In these ancient songs, I read my reality reflected back to me, and I imagined the songwriters as women.

"I lift up my eyes to the hills; from where will my help come? My help comes from the LORD, who made heaven and earth."[2]

"Even though I walk through the darkest valley, I fear no evil, for You are with me."[3]

"Be still, and know that I am God!"[4]

The sacred text offered me sacred hope, and it was with these songs and stories that I began to dig my way up and out. I changed my email and phone number. I encouraged my parents to do the same. I spoke with the district attorney of my hometown to put measures in place for my protection. I slowly began to breathe more deeply. I found a therapist . . .and I gently began to rest.

While the Psalms offered me an entry into the biblical text and into my sacred imagination, I did not stop there. Once I began to imagine women as the singers, women as the writers, women as the storytellers, I saw them everywhere—and they comforted and healed me.

---

[2] Psalm 121:1–2, *New Revised Standard Version*.

[3] Psalm 23:4, *New Revised Standard Version*.

[4] Psalm 46:10, *New Revised Standard Version*.

Healing is never linear. From the moment we're born to the day we die, it is our work to heal, to remember the love from which we came, and to go about dancing, living, and dreaming in that love. Because we don't remember this love all on our own, we always heal in community with others.

Women from the Bible, the ones named and the ones unnamed, joined my community of healing. They whispered their stories to me, and I began to see that I was not alone. I was not the only one abused and terrorized, shamed and undone. I was not the only one with a broken heart, longing to be made whole.

The prayer I pray to myself and my God before I preach, speak, and lead is this: "Make me an instrument of Your peace." Though tradition attributes these words to St. Francis of Assisi, I imagine them coming from St. Clare, Francis's devotee who, when a man yanked her away from the Eucharist table by her long hair because (wait for it) the table was allegedly no place for a woman to be, she promptly cut her hair off and returned to the table to pray, worship, and receive the bread and wine—body and blood of Jesus.

As I pray this prayer, I think of peace not as without conflict, rage, astonishment, or turmoil; rather, I think of peace as standing on sacred and ancient ground *amid all* conflict, rage, astonishment, and turmoil. I ask God to make me an instrument of peace that speaks truth, challenges systems, uproots the lies, and dares to transform that which is into that which might be.

In the beginning there I was: bright-eyed and hungry, screaming for my mother's breast, longing for her skin. I was born with a voice and a vision, a word and a prayer, a clarity and a sacred story birthed from women's stories throughout time, for I would not exist without them. Indeed, none of us would. Into the interconnected stories of women, we enter. Here, we listen, we pray, we identify, we honor.

ONE

Elizabeth

Help Me Grow
Luke 1:5-24, 26, 39-56
Content Warning: Fertility/Infertility

HERSTORY

But they were childless because Elizabeth was not able to conceive.[5]

I was a mother before I was a mother.

My grandmother handed me a date seed when I was eight and said, "Plant this. Watch it grow."

Every day thereafter I checked on the seed, made sure weeds didn't choke it out, knelt in the brown earth, and prayed, "God of my grandmother, help this tree grow."

The seed grew into the palm tree that fed us and healed us, that provided shade from the hot sun and a sign of hope in a dry, broken land.

As I grew and changed, married and moved, the date tree remained steady and true. Zechariah and I were married under the tree and enjoyed its luscious fruit drenched in honey at our wedding feast.

After the wedding, we hoped for a child. But the days turned into months, the months into years, and I had no child to show for being married and sexually active with my husband, something that often became burdensome instead of joyful, a task to complete instead of a love to make.

---

[5] Luke 1:7, *New International Version.*

So that the grief wouldn't swallow me whole, I used to walk the three miles from our home to the date tree's shade, fall on my knees before it as I did when I was a little girl, and pray, "God of my grandmother, help me grow."

My tears watered its roots, muddying the ground beneath me, a portrait of what I thought my life had become. I used to stare into the muddied ground and beg the God of my grandmother, "Please, bring my child to me."

Sorrow became my best friend. For me, it was a particular kind of torture to long for something so intensely, then be reminded that it doesn't yet exist by discovering, month after month, my blood leaving my body. With every cycle of the moon, I'd experience a personal cycle of hope and despair, love and loathing.

The months wore on. The grief cut deeper. *I will not survive this*, I thought. *This will be the month the sorrow will kill me.* Yet I always lived, though I became increasingly more worn out than the month before.

One day, sitting beneath the date tree's shade, I began to whisper:

Dear son,

I love you and I miss you.

The world is different with you not here, and I don't know if you're supposed to be here or somewhere else. I'm trying the best I can to honor wherever and however you may be.

Mostly, I feel a slow, deep ache of longing for you. I want to hold you and love you and feed you and hear you. I want to bask in your wisdom and light. I want you to teach me and lead me. Son, I want to follow.

I never doubted that John the Baptizer was real; he simply hadn't arrived yet but was as real as the sweat and blood pouring from my body. So I began to believe that I was a mother whether I ever grew a baby in my body or not. Society's understanding of fertile and infertile, mother and not a mother were not necessarily wrong, just limited, shallow, untested in the court of real, lived experience.

For I never understood myself as infertile, and I resisted that label for years. My mother, sisters, cousins, midwives, men—all of them called me barren, unable to conceive. But what of Zechariah? What part did he have to play in the making of a child? Why did the blame rest solely on me and my body?

Further, why dismiss the creations I'd conceived other than a human child? The date tree I continued to mother and nurture. The pottery I made with my hands from earth and water. The nieces and nephews I taught how to milk the goats. The husband I loved. The family I fed.

The reality that my body had yet to grow another human felt secondary to the reality that my heart remained wide open to love, which seemed to me to be the most fertile place I could be. And there was something of the God of my grandmother that was persistent in reminding me that openness and love were the very beginnings of anything worth keeping alive.

So as I walked to the date tree every few days to tend and weed and cry and pray, I began to grow not a child, but a life. And that life, I was convinced, is what would lead me to John.

* * *

After this Elizabeth became pregnant and for five months remained in seclusion.[6]

I knew I was pregnant before the angel revealed it to Zechariah, though I was grateful the angel of mercy showed up for him when she did. His heart was broken too.

So often these stories erase men's emotions, pretending that they don't hurt and cry and lament and rage just as much as women. What violence has been done in the name of masculinity, we may never know. What I do know is that Zechariah felt deeply and longed deeply and joined me in the sorrow, though at times it felt as if that sorrow would tear us apart. The more we learned to embrace our grief as a friend, the closer we drew to each other. The more we learned to give voice to our pain, the more we healed.

---

[6] Luke 1:24, *New International Version*.

Once again, I was sitting underneath the date tree. My blood was a week late. Could it be? Laughter filled my throat. What a wonder! What a grace!

My hands found their way to the space just below my belly button. Soft, supple skin. I could imagine a tiny heartbeat beating to the rhythm of my own. I took a deep breath in through my nose and exhaled a long, knowing sigh. Looking up to the tree, lush with fruit, it was as if she smiled at me and said, *You know. I know. We know.*

I bowed my head at her roots, a deep and long thank you, then stood and walked slowly home.

* * *

In the sixth month of Elizabeth's pregnancy, Gabriel visited Mary... Then, Mary hurried to a town in the hill country of Judea to visit Elizabeth.[7]

Immediately, I sent word to my cousin Mary that I was pregnant. When I was six months along, she showed up on my doorstep, sweaty and bedraggled, gracious and kind.

I fetched her a cup of water and smiled at her presence. I knew neither of us would walk this motherhood journey alone.

The scriptures say my baby leapt with joy at her presence, which is true. What is also true is that *I* leapt with joy at her presence, gratitude coursing through my veins. My baby took my cue, sensing the jubilation of solidarity, the rapture of hearts and bodies connected, the relief of physical presence. Our collective joy poured up and out of our hearts and into melody and music.

My song echoed the songs of countless women before us who knew what it was to stand side by side, blessing and believing one another against all odds:

Blessed are you among women. . . Blessed is she who has believed.[8]

Mary's song joined the chorus of the prophets, heralding the God who feeds and upends for the sake of love, foreshadowing the

---

[7] Luke 1:26, 39, *New International Version* and *New Revised Standard Version*.
[8] Luke 1:42, 45, *New International Version*.

life-altering work our children would one day undertake. Mary's song was the song of our grandmothers, and it was the song we sang daily, sometimes hourly, as our bellies grew and as we waited for the world to turn.

* * *

Mary stayed with Elizabeth for about three months and then returned home.[9]

Here's what happens: A small cramp just below the abdomen signals it is time. The cramp grows to an ache, intensifying every few minutes. By the end, you're doing well to breathe. "Get this baby out!" you scream.

Though you know you were made for this, the mindful mantras no longer satisfy. Only a baby out of your vagina and screaming upon your breast will do.

Three pushes and he was out, thank God! The lad was screaming sermons from the start.

I held him upon my chest, too tired to cry. As he latched onto my left breast, I looked up, my eyes catching Mary's. Because she'd stayed with us for three months, she was present for the birth of John the Baptist. She held my hand. She sang me songs. She helped me breathe.

As our eyes locked, tears formed like waves behind her eyes. She never uttered a word. She didn't have to. I knew. The thin line between life and death that's always present in the birthing room shook her to her core. Though she held my hand in one of hers, her other hand held her belly. A look of terror and delight spanned her face, anticipating her own deliverance of Jesus in a few short months.

I refused to look away. *Stay with me,* my eyes said. *Stay with me.*

We stared at each other for no more than sixty seconds that blessed day, sixty seconds that felt like sixty years. Before turning back toward baby John, we leaned toward each other. Our foreheads met, the tips of our noses touched, our eyes closed, our breath matched.

---

[9] Luke 1:56, *New International Version.*

Offering a blessing as only sisters can, it was as if we were saying to each other: *Your life matters too.*

It was as if we knew the energy, gravitas, and emotion each of our sons would require. Both were beautiful and worthy, no doubt, yet nevertheless exhausting and time-consuming, heart-wrenching and nerve-racking for their mothers.

We knew the power a simple blessing could sustain. It was as if we were made not so much for motherhood, but for sisterhood, a tethering to the very best of each other for life and for whatever lay beyond.

Before parting, we whispered our sister-prayer: "God of our grandmothers, help us heal."

"Blessed are you among women, I said. *Blessed is she who has believed."*

LITURGY FOR MORNING PRAYER

Inspired by Elizabeth's Song from Luke 1:42–45

OPENING

If you are gathered with others, position yourselves in a circle. Place a candle in the center. If you are alone, light a candle as a sign of connection to the circle of women saints who join you, even now, as you pray.

Morning Confession

Blessed are the women.

Blessed is she who believes.

Morning Prayer of Gratitude

For the women who, throughout time, have kept us alive with their relentless believing, we give thanks.

For the women who, throughout time, have sustained us with their determined practice of joy, we give thanks.

For the women who, throughout time, have joined one another in song, dance, and jubilation, we give thanks.

For their mercy, for their grace, for their connection, for their love, we praise you, O God of our grandmothers. Amen.

Morning Psalm | Psalm 18:1–3 (inspired by the Common English Bible translation)

I love you, Sovereign, my strength.

You are my solid rock, my womb, my Deliverer.

My God is my ground. I take refuge in my God.

You are my heart and my place of safety.

Because you are praiseworthy, I cry out to you.

You deliver me, time and again, from all my fears.

Scripture Reading: Luke 1:5-24, 26, 39-56

The word of life.

Thanks be to the God of our grandmothers.

Silence

Prayers of the People

For women everywhere, who are living amid war . . .

For women everywhere, who are giving birth . . .

For women everywhere, who are feeding their families . . .

For women everywhere, who are leading in loving ways . . .

For women everywhere, who are longing to be heard . . .

For women everywhere, who are speaking words that are sometimes hard to hear . . .

For women everywhere, who are stitching scraps of fabric together to make a blanket, to make a life . . .

For women everywhere, who . . . *(Follow with your own prayer for women throughout the world, for women in your own life, for women who beckon us to believe.)*

Loving God, we give You thanks.

Merciful God, hear our prayers.

Amen.

Song of Praise

"Blessed Is She"

Words and music by Claire K. McKeever-Burgett

The following song can be sung several times through in the practice of meditative singing, the repetition of which offers a deeper connection to God and to the women who are to be followed and whose stories are to be believed.

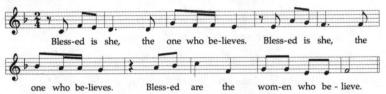

Bless-ed is she, the one who be-lieves. Bless-ed is she, the
one who be-lieves. Bless-ed are the wom-en who be - lieve.

Contemporary Connection[10]

Take a few moments to watch and listen to "A Beautiful Noise" by Alicia Keys and Brandi Carlile.[11] Imagine Elizabeth and Mary singing this together.

The Prayer of Mary (inspired by Luke 1:46–55)[12]

O Mother God, we glorify You.

From the depths of our beings, we rejoice in You,

---

[10] The *Contemporary Connection* is a reminder that our worship is not meant to be divorced from our everyday lives but is meant to transform and accompany them, revealing to us that the Holy is everywhere and in everything, even and especially in the music we may not traditionally associate with "church." Perhaps these modern links will also inspire you to dance, sing, and play as a part of your daily spiritual practice and not separate from it.

[11] www.youtube.com/watch?v=_yU1x-p_OdY.

[12] Every liturgy in this book includes three elements: *The Prayer of Mary*, inspired by her song in Luke 1:46–55; *a simple chorus* I wrote inspired by Elizabeth's song in the first chapter, entitled, "Blessed Is She"; and a *Contemporary Connection*, which is a link to a current song and/or video that relates to the woman in each chapter.

The Prayer of Mary takes the place of the *Prayer of Jesus* (commonly known as *The Lord's Prayer*), which is traditionally prayed at the end of each daily liturgy. "Blessed Is She" is a meditative singing moment in which we sing the same few words repetitively as a means of prayer and connection to God and to the women. The simple tune is one I've been singing to my children for many years now, introducing different words to suit the seasons of our lives.

Our Deliverer.

As You show mercy to us, help us show mercy to others.

As You honor our bodies, help us honor all other bodies.

As You scatter the deceitful and remove tyrants from their thrones,

help us work for justice and shalom.

Fill the hungry with good things.

Show us what is enough.

Deliver us from pride into mercy.

Deliver us from evil into love.

For yours is the birthing room, the power, the vulnerability,

the glory, and the love,

eternally here, eternally now.

Amen.

Benediction

May we go forth from this place, believing women, and in believing them, blessing them now and forevermore.
Amen.

REFLECTION AND CURIOSITY

The following questions are meant to deepen and expand, invite and beckon your thoughtful, compassionate, curious responses to the story and liturgy of Elizabeth. Whether engaging these questions on your own or in a group setting, carve out space for journaling, collaging, or painting in response. If engaging in a group discussion, choose one or two questions, at most, to hold at the center of your sacred circle.

1. In what ways does your story connect with Elizabeth's story? What resonates? What makes you curious?

2. When reading and praying along with Elizabeth, what sensations do you notice in your body?

3. What is your understanding of sisterhood or siblinghood? In what ways has sisterhood/siblinghood shown itself in your life, and with whom?

4. Who is the God of your grandmothers? Who is the God you follow?

5. What do you know about fertility/infertility? What is the common narrative you've heard about infertility? What is a narrative you *want* to hear about fertility/infertility?

6. What would it mean to regard even your pain as holy and sacred?

PUBLIC WITNESS

One of the most powerful ways I've experienced blessing is with other women and mothers as we sit together in sacred circles to tell our stories, ask for help, and, in so doing, heal. It is a powerful, tangible act of togetherness that reminds us repeatedly that we are not alone.

The story and language of Elizabeth and her sister-cousin, Mary, lead me to the real-life work of:

Chamber of Mothers, a nonprofit focusing America's priorities on mothers' rights through grassroots movements, local chapters, and community-building. Chamber of Mothers seeks to unite mothers as advocates to create the country we want to live in and bestow upon future generations.

Raphah Institute, a nonprofit organization working toward the holistic well-being of young children, their families, and their communities by supporting healing and restorative early childhood learning.

Learn more about these organizations and programs, and discover more about organizations in your area doing the work of community-building, family advocacy, and familial and generational healing. Connect. Learn. Give. Grow.[13]

---

[13] https://www.chamberofmothers.com/ and https://www.raphah.org/

Two

Mary

The First Supper

Luke 2:1–20

Content Warning: Birth

HERSTORY

And she pondered all of these things in her heart.[14]

It was quiet but for the bleating of a goat and the soft suckle of your lips on my nipple, the First Supper. Your father slept in the corner of the barn on a pillow of hay. After stitching my body where it tore, Dinah, my midwife, left, weary from attending my long, slow labor.

I lay awake, bleeding, and desperate for something to take away the pain. The experience of labor is like wave upon wave of hell. Once the baby has left the body, there comes a new wave, a softer one, but still a wave crashing upon the shore, whispering quietly, "You survived . . . but just barely."

Every cell tingles with this awareness and shudders at the thought of it. Death was so close I could taste it. But then life was so close too. Does the body quake at the reality of them both? You can't have one without the other.

I was so tired all I could do was lie there and stare, acutely aware of my surroundings and simultaneously unhinged from this earth, floating up and beyond whatever life this was, whatever lives we had become.

---

[14] Luke 2:19.

I remember the smell of lavender and blood. Both soothed me—lavender with its sweet and calming scent; blood with its awakening.

I didn't cry when I first saw you; I only gasped, desperate for air. Though I labored for hours, the moment of your arrival earthside came like a shot. Dinah and your father had to tear you from me; that's how reluctant either of us were to let go.

Covered in blood—was it yours or mine or both of ours?—they placed you on my chest. You screamed. I marveled: *I created this?*

Dark hair. Dark eyes. Whoever said there is no light in the darkness? Because you illumined that night with your darkness, and I began to see that making our way in the dark is all there ever is. I began to see darkness as beautiful. You taught me this, dear one. You.

Your father wasn't meant to be there. Matters of labor and birth, blood and uterus were typically withheld from men, thought to be spaces where only women dwelt, spaces understood as unclean. Yet there he was, holding my hand, watching me bleed—another one of the night's tiny miracles. Your father—presently, patiently—helped me bring you into this world.

I had a month left before I thought you'd arrive. The plan was to be back at home so that my mother-in-law and sisters could tend to me as I rode wave upon wave of contraction and pain.

Plans are for fools. Wisdom laughs in their faces. In the end, all we have is a hope and a prayer, a kneeling down and a letting go.

They say shepherds visited us that night, but their visit came later, after the days of cleansing had passed, when the law considered me pure again. How I could be considered impure after bringing you into this world is beyond me. Through sweat and blood, through broken flesh and tilting bone, it is all pure power to me.

No, that night, it was just us. And a host of mother saints cheering us on, bidding me, "Push," and holding you, "Hush."

That was the first night I remember thinking: *I am never alone, no matter how alone I may feel.* This same thought would return to me throughout your life—at your leaving, your preaching, your dying. What of this didn't break me in two?

It was as if your birth prepared me to rely on Mother God and gave me practice for what was to come, the foreboding of the body-breaking, blood-shedding miracle that you were only able to endure because I endured it first.

Of course, none of this was coherent the night you were born. All that was clear was you and your darkening light as you suckled my breast. Only me and my stinging, dull pain. Only my body and yours, bruised and bloodied, lying on the floor of a nameless barn on the outskirts of Bethlehem. With a bleating goat and a soft snore from your father.

It was there that not only you were made; I was made too. Not so much as your mother (though that was a title I claimed joyfully), but more as a survivor, as one who came face-to-face with death and lived.[15]

LITURGY FOR NIGHT PRAYER

OPENING

If you are gathered with others, position yourselves in a circle. Place a candle in the center. If you are alone, light a candle as a sign of connection to the circle of women saints who join you, even now, as you pray.

Opening Prayer

On this Holy Night, Mother God, we pray together in the spirit of young Mary, whose song echoes throughout Jesus' ministry, whose fire and passion, conviction and grace lead us to light and life. Help us turn the world upside down. Help us join in the groans of labor to bring forth life anew. Help us fan the flames of your justice. Help us burn what needs burning. Help us mend what needs mending. And on this most holy of nights, help us honor Mary and all who mother the world into love. **Amen.**

Silence

---

[15] Parts of Mary's story and liturgy below first appeared in *The Other Journal,* December 13, 2021.

Prayer of Confession

Mother God who sustained Mary, who sustains us all—

We confess that we have done a poor job of caring for mothers, of listening to and holding them, of honoring and celebrating their stories, of bowing down at the feet of those who bring us into the world and keep it spinning. We confess that without Mary we would not have Jesus. We confess that without Jesus we would not truly live.

Forgive us, O God of Mary, for our ignorance and our disregard, and help us to follow the light of the flame into places that honor and bless the ones from whom we come, the bodies, broken, from which we burst forth. Help us honor. Help us love. Help us, Mother God, we pray.

Forgiveness + Grace

God shows mercy to everyone, from one generation to the next. Thanks be to Mary. Thanks be to God. **Alleluia! Amen.**

Psalm 96 (inspired by the Common English Bible translation)

O sing a new song!

Sing a song

of bearing forth new life,

of being saved by the God of Mary.

Declare the God of Mary's glory everywhere—

in birthing rooms and at communion tables,

on deathbeds and at riversides.

Families of all kinds,

rest in God's gentleness and strength;

trust that you are safe in the God of Mary's

loving presence.

Say to everyone, "The God of Mary is among us!

Though the earth moves, Her love remains.

Though the nations war, Her peace remains.

Though the women suffer, Her joy remains."

Both heaven and earth dance together before
the God of Mary.

**The seas sing, the fields undulate, the trees sway–
the God of Mary is coming
with pleasure, with ease, with comfort, with love.**

Psalm Prayer

We rest this holy night in the God of Mary, entrusting
our lives to Her love. **Amen.**

Scripture Reading: Luke 2:1–20

Silence for Reflection

Song of Praise

"Blessed Is She"
Words and music by Claire K. McKeever-Burgett

*The following song can be sung several times following the practice of
meditative singing, the repetition of which offers a deeper connection to
God and to the women who are to be followed and whose stories are to
be believed.*

Bless-ed is she, the one who be-lieves. Bless-ed is she, the one who be-lieves. Bless-ed are the wom-en who be-lieve.

Contemporary Connection

*Take a few moments to watch and listen to "Mary" by Patty Griffin,
performed by Patty Griffin and Natalie Maines.[16] Imagine Mary singing
this song to her child, Jesus.*

---

[16] https://www.youtube.com/watch?v=XOxpvKuEruk

The Prayer of Mary (inspired by Luke 1:46–55)

O Mother God, we glorify You.

From the depths of our beings, we rejoice in You,

Our Deliverer.

As You show mercy to us, help us to show mercy to others.

As You honor our bodies, help us to honor all other bodies.

As You scatter the deceitful and remove tyrants from their thrones,

help us to work for justice and shalom.

Fill the hungry with good things.

Show us what is enough.

Deliver us from pride into mercy.

Deliver us from evil into love.

For Yours is the birthing room, the power, the vulnerability,

the glory, and the love,

eternally here, eternally now.

Amen.

Silence

Depart in peace and quiet to love and serve women and the world. Amen.

REFLECTION AND CURIOSITY

The following questions are meant to deepen and expand, invite and beckon thoughtful, compassionate, curious responses to the story and liturgy of Mary. Whether playing with these questions on your own or in a group setting, carve out space for journaling, collaging, or painting in response. If engaging in a group discussion, choose one or two questions, at most, to hold at the center of your sacred circle.

1. What thoughts and feelings arise when reading Mary's birthing story? In what ways does your story connect with Mary's story?

2. When reading and praying along with Mary, what sensations do you notice in your body?

3. What is it like to pray to Mother God?

4. What do you know about how you came into the world? What is your birth story?

PUBLIC WITNESS

Black mothers and birthing people often do not receive the care they need and deserve when trying to get pregnant, when giving birth, and when healing afterward. Birth justice is about changing this reality.

Black Mamas Matter Alliance is a powerful, Black-women-led organization that centers Black mamas and birthing people in advocacy, research, power-building, and culture-shifting for Black parental health, rights, and justice.

On a global scale, **Every Mother Counts** seeks to make pregnancy and childbirth safe for every mother, everywhere.

Learn more about these organizations and programs, and discover more about organizations in your area doing the work of advocacy, research, empowerment, and care for Black maternal health. Connect. Learn. Give. Grow.[17]

---

[17] https://blackmamasmatter.org/ and https://everymothercounts.org/

THREE

Anna

Prophet, Poet, Priest

Luke 2:36–38

HERSTORY

There was also a prophet, Anna.[18]

There's something liberating about growing old. No longer desirable to men; no longer envied by women. An invisibility can cloak an old woman's shoulders, setting her free.

This is how it was for me. An old, invisible woman holding vigil, beholden to nothing but my prayer and the belief that God would show up.

I made my bed on the temple floor, comforted by a mat and some straw, waking every two hours to pray. Following the prayers of my ancestors, I would simply sing: "Dwelling Place, send your child, and set us free."

We—Jews, women, poor—were oppressed by the empire, pawns in a system designed *by* wealthy men *for* wealthy men. Where, I wondered, was the hope for the rest of us?

* * *

Only seven years into my marriage, my husband died. Our marriage was like many marriages in ancient Israel: at the age of eighteen, I was married to a man ten years my senior. When my husband died,

---

[18] Luke 2:36, *New Revised Standard Version.*

I returned home to my father, Phanuel, to be looked after for the rest of my days.

I lived a simple life: milking goats, dyeing fabrics to sell at market, sweeping the earthen floors. Through household chores, I learned the art of praying: repetition and release. Showing up, doing the work, letting God take care of the rest.

Years of practice emptying buckets, dyeing fabrics, and milking goats qualified me to enter the holy temple. There, I made my simple abode in the very dwelling place of God, even though long ago I learned to meet God everywhere.

My entry into the temple was not because I thought God was only to be found there. Quite the opposite: I entered the temple because God's presence everywhere gave me the confidence to meet God, even and especially there.

At the age of eighty, I was easy enough to ignore . . . until Mary gave birth to Jesus. Her labor to bring that dark-haired, soulful boy into the world sparked a fire in me like no other birth had.

On the night of his birth, I woke with a start. The vision of her body broken open in labor was so close to the vision of God, the Deliverer, the One Who Gives Birth, I almost thought it might be the same vision I'd been having for years. But something felt different. The air was ripe, and the stars aligned. The spirits danced. I was too old not to trust my gut. Jesus, because of Mary, was being born.

Rolling out my mat, I kneeled and began to pray: "Dwelling Place, send your child, and set us free."

It was a hum and a rock, a meditation song of old. When women sing, our vibrations join with the groans and vibrations of the whole earth, helping it come to life again and again. In this way, each of us plays a part in the birth of a new world. All we must do is open our mouths and let the melody come forth.

Rocking and humming, singing and laughing, I woke the entire temple that night. Jesus, God's very own, was being born.

When the time came for the purification rituals, Mary, Joseph, and Jesus visited the temple. I slipped Mary some soothing herbs for her and her family's continued healing.

"My prayers are with you," I said. "Prayers of gratitude. Prayers of healing."

She glanced at me with a knowing look, a sadness mixed with joy and a sense of being overwhelmed, the look a new mother holds in every line of her face, every fold of her skin. Though I had never birthed children of my own, I could imagine the exhaustion and the elation of new parenthood. And if you can imagine something, it becomes real.

As they left, I sang the song I'd been singing for years, but with new words: "Dwelling Place, you've sent your child to us. We are free. We are free. We are free."

I danced that day and the next and the next. No priest in the temple could deny the power of Jesus' and Mary's presence. There'd been a shift in the earth's foundation, and we all felt it deep in our bones.

Who else had the power to disrupt entire governments other than the Mother and Child of God?

* * *

A few weeks later, I took my final breath on earth, and joined the great mysterious beyond.

I only knew Mary and Jesus for a short time on this earth, but I like to think I knew them much longer. One of the gifts of being a prophet is that in visions we see what is possible, what is real. For in this mother and her child, God, our Dwelling Place, showed us a way of living that can set us and the whole world free.

I continue to sing in the great mysterious beyond, joining a chorus of saints and sinners who keep alive the prayer for freedom: "Dwelling Place, send your child, and set us free."

We practice our faith again and again, through singing, through child-bearing-and-birthing, through following and leading, through listening and through cleaning, hoping and trusting that the practice will eventually set us free.

LITURGY FOR MIDDAY PRAYER

OPENING

If you are gathered with others, position yourselves in a circle. Place a candle in the center. If you are alone, light a candle as a sign of connection to the circle of women saints who join you, even now, as you pray.

Call to Prayer

> **God, in you we find a safe dwelling,**
>
> A place to pause, breathe, and give thanks.

Prayer at Midday

> **Shekinah, Dwelling Place, God—**
>
> **This midday pause reminds us of Your mercy.**
>
> **Everything we have done, everything we will do is Yours.**
>
> **Our work is Your work. Our witness is Your witness.**
>
> **May it be whole. May it be loving. May it be just.**
>
> **Amen.**

Psalm 84 (inspired by the Common English Bible translation)

> Your dwelling place is beautiful, O God,
>
> Your dwelling place is You.
>
> **Wherever a sparrow makes a home for her young;**
>
> **Wherever a river makes its way down a mountain;**
>
> **Wherever the sun shines and the rains fall,**
>
> **This is where we want to be.**
>
> Your dwelling place is beautiful, O God;
>
> Your dwelling place is You.
>
> **Amen.**

Pause here for a moment of silence.

Song of Praise

"Blessed Is She"
Words and music by Claire K. McKeever-Burgett

The following song can be sung several times through in the practice of meditative singing, the repetition of which offers a deeper connection to God and to the women who are to be followed and whose stories are to be believed.

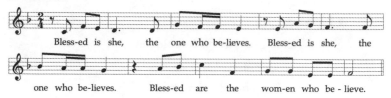

Bless-ed is she, the one who be-lieves. Bless-ed is she, the one who be-lieves. Bless-ed are the wom-en who be - lieve.

Contemporary Connection

Take a few moments to watch and listen to "Freedom" by Beyoncé.[19] You may also find yourself wanting to dance while listening to this song. If you do, then please dance! Imagine Anna singing this song as her prophetic witness to freedom.

The Prayer of Mary (inspired by Luke 1:46–55)

O Mother God, we glorify You.

From the depths of our beings, we rejoice in You,

Our Deliverer.

As You show mercy to us, help us to show mercy to others.

As You honor our bodies, help us to honor all other bodies.

As You scatter the deceitful and remove tyrants from their thrones,

help us also to work for justice and shalom.

Fill the hungry with good things.

Show us what is enough.

---

[19] https://www.youtube.com/watch?v=4eX23_HoRbM

Deliver us from pride into mercy.

Deliver us from evil into love.

For Yours is the birthing room, the power, the vulnerability,

the glory, and the love,

eternally here, eternally now.

Amen.

Closing Blessing

May the shelter You provide embolden us,

not to hide away from the world,

but to engage it, embrace it, and love it,

trusting that when we dwell in You,

we dwell in Love.

Amen.

REFLECTION AND CURIOSITY

The following questions are meant to deepen and expand, invite and beckon thoughtful, compassionate, curious responses to the story and liturgy of Anna. Whether playing with these questions on your own or in a group setting, carve out space for journaling, collaging, or painting in response. If engaging in a group discussion, choose one or two questions, at most, to hold at the center of your sacred circle.

1. In what ways does your story connect with Anna's story? What resonates with you? What draws you in?

2. When reading and praying along with Anna, what sensations did you notice in your body?

3. Recall a time when you learned from a woman leader. What did you learn? What did you feel while learning from her?

4. What would the world look like if there were more women leaders?

5. What barriers exist for women in the church? In what ways can you help remove these barriers?

6. What would it look like to claim your authority now and not wait for old age or undesirability?

PUBLIC WITNESS

I'll never forget when my boyfriend shared with his father and brother an argumentative essay I'd written in college on the case for women in leadership in the church. It was only when they responded with affirmations regarding how well-written and well-argued the essay was that he told them it was penned by me. Later, when he told me he'd sent the essay to them without my name on it, I was aghast and struggled to find the words to express my shock and disgust at his removal of my name from something I wrote. The irony of making public an essay about women's leadership in the church without the writer's name is both laughable and lamentable, yet another sign of how we women get ignored and erased from the narrative.

What I remember arguing in the essay then is what I continue to argue today: women in every denomination and every church house *must* preach, lead, pastor, and prophesy if we want communities to heal. To deny women the opportunity to lead is to deny our churches and communities, our children and ourselves the gifts and graces of more than half of the world's population. Women are not liabilities; we are leaders.

Women's Ordination has been the uncompromising feminist voice for women's ordination and gender equity within the Roman Catholic Church since 1975. The group's collective vision is of a Roman Catholic Church that affirms women's gifts, responds by calling them to ministry and ordination, openly and actively supports women's voices, and reflects the example of Jesus by welcoming all to the table.

WomanPreach! Inc. seeks to produce a network of preachers who will use their voices in service to the Gospel of Jesus Christ, especially as it relates to womanist/feminist concerns of equity and justice, for the sake of the salvation and freedom of all.

Learn more about these organizations, and discover organizations and faith communities in your area doing the work of advocacy, affirmation, empowerment, and training for women church leaders, pastors, and preachers. Connect. Learn. Give. Grow.[20]

FOUR

Eve

The "Sinful" Woman
Luke 7:36–50

HERSTORY

Meanwhile, a woman from the city, a sinner, discovered that Jesus was dining in the Pharisee's house.[21]

I was humming a song as I arrived at the dinner party that night, deep and low, melodic and mesmerizing.

You know the night because you've read about it in Scripture. Some versions of the story label me as "the sinful woman"; others offer a softer header, like "forgiveness and gratitude."

If it were me telling the story (and I suppose I am now!), I'd title the whole affair "Questioned and Questioning Woman." I'd also make sure you all know my name.

I am Eve. Yes, you heard me right. My mom thought it was a beautiful and good idea to name me after the first woman. Our name means "living," after all, from the Hebrew word *havah*, which literally means "to breathe, to live, to give life."

And after the long labor my mama endured to bring me into this world, the name Eve became my mother's declaration of my living and of hers too.

As beautiful and profound as my mom thought the name was, it wasn't easy walking around with the name of the woman who bore the first scarlet letter, the mark of shame, the label of sinner.

---

[21] Luke 7:37, *Common English Bible.*

Nevertheless, I stood proud as a girl named Eve. I took care of my sisters (we never had any brothers). I milked the goats and swept the floor and helped Mama with dinner and welcomed Papa home after his long fishing trips out at sea.

Yet everything changed one morning when Papa didn't return home. I was fifteen. His friend and fellow fisherman showed up at the doorstep to say Papa had been caught in a storm out on the boat, thrown overboard, and was never seen again.

Shock paralyzed all of us. If it weren't for the sounds of Mama's wailing, I might not have believed it was true. But something within me told me it was, and that life would never be the same.

You see, Papa didn't have any brothers, and his parents were already dead. And in our culture, you had to have a man to take care of you. Women didn't work. Well, we worked plenty, but we weren't paid for our work the way men were paid for theirs. So with news of Papa's death, it fell to me, the eldest daughter with nothing but younger sisters and a mother, to care for the family.

I suppose you could say this is how I "fell into sin." With no formal education, because I was a girl, and no fishing crew willing to take a woman on their boat, I was left with few options that would bring in the money needed to sustain my family.

It has always felt a bit odd to me, the shame that we women must carry because of a society that cares so little for us.

Nevertheless, to save my family, I sold my body to the men who required it. And instead of the men who used me night after night bearing the shame of their desire, I carried it with the label of "sinful woman."

Looking back, my questions are what saved me. Lying on the floor after the men left, I would let my curiosity transport me elsewhere.

Why must I bear the shame of their desire? Why must it be my fault that this is all I can do to feed my sisters and my mother? Why must I be considered a sinner while the men who use me are considered blameless?

Where is love? How can I find it? What would it look like to know love and hold love and make love a living thing instead of this?

Despite everyone else in town questioning my character because of how I supported our family, I sustained my own line of questions, and the questions kept me alive.

* * *

"She brought perfumed oil in a vase made of alabaster."[22]

I was in the midst of a daydream of wonder the day I met him, the one about whom I was singing at the beginning: Jesus.

I'd heard about him several months prior, so I knew he came with a crowd of people always following him and begging him for miracles and mercy. He sounded too good to be true.

He looked me in the eyes in pure daylight—something most men would never be caught doing. (My eyes were only to be seen in the dead of night.)

He asked me my name, and when I told him, he said, "Ah, yes. Eve. Giver of life."

It was as if he had known me for years—familiar and mysterious all at once.

Of course, I followed him that night to Simon's house, singing and dancing and dreaming all the way, hoping to love him in a way I hadn't ever loved anyone before.

Again, my questions are the ones that gave me the audacity to follow, to listen, to enter the home (uninvited), to weep, to anoint, to serve.

Why not anoint Jesus? Why not love him with a fierce, unashamed love? When will there ever be this moment again?

With my love and my oil, my tears and my body, I blessed my Jesus.

I knew they'd question me. I knew they'd call me a sinful woman . . . or worse. I knew they'd question him for accepting my gift, my oil, my love.

But I no longer cared.

My oil was ready. My tears abundant. My blessing real.

---

[22] Luke 7:37, *Common English Bible.*

True to his character, Jesus defended me. Jesus saw me. The real me. Not the woman of the night or the woman full of sin. But me—Eve, giver of life. He recognized my extravagance as a gift. He accepted my anointing as love.

Then, in what felt like a dramatic turn of events, Jesus looked me in the eyes again, this time in front of a crowd of men who otherwise would have condemned and hidden me forever to live in shame.

Yes, he looked me in the eyes and said: "You are forgiven. Your faith has saved you. Now, be at peace."

Simon and the others gasped with indignity. I gasped with joy.

With a few simple words, Jesus confirmed what I'd always sensed was true: I was loved. Not in spite of my life but because of it. Not in spite of my questions but because of them. Shame lives where it is kept hidden and secret, lurking and afraid. Now, standing in the full light of love, the shame men attributed to me because of how they used my body was no longer hidden. Fully illuminated, I stood up on my own two feet—shoulders back, eyes open—and smiled.

"I am not the sum of your shame," I said to the room full of men. "The peace Jesus bestows is the peace I rightfully claim. Peace with who I am: Eve, giver of life. This is who I've always been."

There were other women who followed him, who funded his ministry and work, without whom there'd have been no ministry and no miracles. Mary. Susanna. Joanna. They were waiting for me, arms wide open, as I left the Pharisee's house that night.

They said, "You are welcome here. So are your mother and your sisters. Come, join our circle and our ministry. Here, you will be cared for and free."

So we joined Jesus' followers, traveling through cities and villages to proclaim the good news of the kingdom of God. This was the salvation Jesus gave me. Community. Being introduced to other women and other work, being taught alternative skills and trades, being fed and clothed, given shelter and housing apart from what my body and my beauty could afford my family and me.

See, the problem was never me. The problem was (and perhaps still is) a world that treats people as commodities, that demands we sell ourselves for the sake of survival. The problem is a world that tries to disconnect people from people, dismantling communities and disenfranchising us from ourselves. When we build community and connect to ourselves and others in ways that help us ask questions and discover new ways of being and living, we challenge the systems that be (the status quo). While that can be terrifying for the people in power, it is liberating (full of forgiveness and love) for us.

My body became the source of my strength and my power as it showed up in the circle of women day after day after day. In the circle, my body learned that it was valued not for its appearance but for its existence; not for what it could do but simply for who it was—me. My body learned, through time and practice, that it was safe. How many loaves did I knead? How many pots did I stir? How many threads did I sew? How many meals did I share before every bone and cell in my body knew it was holy and safe?

"Healing is an ongoing practice," the women would always say, reminding me that it would take time and presence to get there.

After all, my questions, which are part of my practice and my healing, are what led me to Jesus—or Jesus to me. My encounter with this most present and direct man freed me to keep singing, dancing, and questioning all along the way.

Historians and theologians have written about me throughout time. Indeed, I've been the subject of many arguments and debates in the church and beyond. Some have said that my anointing of Jesus foreshadowed his death and his anointing in the tomb. Others have said that I created more controversy around Jesus' life and ministry.

But I say I met someone who changed my life, who saw me as Eve, giver of life, and who reminded me of my calling to do just that: to give life—to myself, to my family, and to others.

So I keep asking my questions of a world that tries hard to render me silent. And I keep blessing that which requires a blessing. And I keep following Jesus, who looked me in the eye, called me by my name, and introduced me to women who opened wide the circle of inclusion to welcome in my sisters, mother, and me, declaring me loved, forgiven, whole.

LITURGY FOR NIGHT PRAYER

OPENING

If you are gathered with others, position yourselves in a circle. Place a candle in the center. If you are alone, light a candle as a sign of connection to the circle of women saints who join you, even now, as you pray.

Opening Prayer at the Lighting of the Candles

You are our light and our salvation.

You connect us to one another.

May Your light shine in the darkness.

May Your darkness shine in the light.

May we bask in the beauty of both.

Amen.

Prayer of Confession and Accountability

We confess our complicity in systems that seek to dominate and subjugate women.

For the ways we judge women's bodies, holding them to impossible standards of artificial and conditional constructs of beauty, forgive us.

For the ways we reduce women to particular, limited roles, ignoring them as the whole people that they are, forgive us.

For the times we've witnessed the degradation of women and have said and done nothing, forgive us.

Also, we pray, make us accountable.

When we judge women's bodies, help us create organizations and systems and communities and words that say, "*That is* not acceptable. Here's what *is*."

When we reduce women to a mere role, help us dig deeper and expand our imaginations to tell stories about the complex, confident, confused, dynamic people women truly are.

When we witness the degradation of women and say nothing, give us the words to say *no* and to hold a safe,

healing space for women to find dignity, worth, and repair.

Merciful God, Your mercy begs us to do better. Our confessions are a place to start.

Help us now to rest in Your grace so that we may wake tomorrow renewed for the work of reparation and accountability. Amen.

Psalm 4 (inspired by *Common English Bible* translation)

We are crying in the streets, O God!

We've been maligned for too long!

Set us free from white supremacy and patriarchy!

Listen to our prayers.

How long will we be insulted simply for being who you created us to be?

How long will our communities love what is worthless and pursue lie after lie?

Tonight, we rest in this knowledge: That our God takes care of us.

That She hears us when we cry. She dances with us when we dance.

She rocks and sways and breathes and prays alongside us.

When people say, "A good woman is hard to find,"

We reply, "What do you mean by good? The light of Mother God's face is all the goodness we need. She is with us eternally."

Our hearts are full of joy. Abundance is our birthright.

Therefore, we crawl into bed and fall asleep in peace.

With God alone, we live liberated and free.

Scripture Reading: Luke 7:36–50

A living, breathing word.

Thanks be to God.

Silence

Song of Praise

"Blessed Is She"

Words and music by Claire K. McKeever-Burgett

The following song can be sung several times through in the practice of meditative singing, the repetition of which offers a deeper connection to God and to the women who are to be followed and whose stories are to be believed.

Bless-ed is she, the one who be-lieves. Bless-ed is she, the one who be-lieves. Bless-ed are the wom-en who be - lieve.

Contemporary Connection

Take a few moments to watch and listen to "CHURCH GIRL" by Beyoncé.[23] You may also find yourself wanting to dance while listening to this song, in which case, dance! Imagine Eve singing this song at the dinner table with Jesus and the religious leaders, free from their judgment, free from their shame.

The Prayer of Mary (inspired by Luke 1:46–55)

O Mother God, we glorify You.

From the depths of our beings, we rejoice in You,

Our Deliverer.

As You show mercy to us, help us show mercy to others.

As You honor our bodies, help us honor all other bodies.

As You scatter the deceitful and remove tyrants from their thrones,

help us work for justice and shalom.

Fill the hungry with good things.

Show us what is enough.

Deliver us from pride into mercy.

---

[23] https://www.youtube.com/watch?v=_sZirWKsOBg

Deliver us from evil into love.

For Yours is the birthing room, the power, the
vulnerability,

the glory, and the love,

eternally here, eternally now.

Amen.

Closing Blessing

We are women of the night,

peaceful and abundant,

full of grace and light.

We rest in the bosom of our God,

both when the sun and the moon shine.

Tonight we rest. Tomorrow we wake

to follow You. **Amen.**

REFLECTION AND CURIOSITY

The following questions are meant to deepen and expand, invite and
beckon thoughtful, compassionate, curious responses to the story
and liturgy of Eve. Whether playing with these questions on your
own or in a group setting, carve out space for journaling, collaging,
or painting in response. If engaging in a group discussion, choose one
or two questions, at most, to hold at the center of your sacred circle.

1. In what ways does your story connect with Eve's story? What
    resonates? What draws you in?

2. When reading and praying along with Eve, what sensations do
    you notice in your body?

3. Recall a time when the loving actions of another changed you.
    What did it look like and feel like to be loved?

4. In what ways do you judge women's bodies? How might you
    begin to shed harmful ideologies of womanhood and sexuality?

5. What does freedom look like and feel like for you?

PUBLIC WITNESS

I first encountered the work of **Thistle Farms** while in divinity school. With my class on social justice and the gospel, we visited local nonprofits engaging the work of love. Surrounded by cardboard boxes, bubble wrap, and packing paper—as well as candle wax, wicks, scissors, and other supplies needed to create, pack, and ship their candles around the world—the women of Thistle Farms invited our class to join their opening circle for the day. Similar to a twelve-step meeting, the circle followed a process of speaking aloud our names, hearing a person's story, and then holding space for curiosity, reflection, and connection.

The integrity with which the women sitting in our circle engaged the process struck me. They did not swim in shallow waters; they owned their stories of both pain and healing, which is how and why they were able to share parts of themselves with us. Their willingness to go deep invited me to do the same, and ever since then I've been a follower and supporter of Thistle Farms, a nonprofit social enterprise dedicated to helping women survivors recover and heal from prostitution, trafficking, and addiction by providing a safe place to live, a meaningful job, and a lifelong sisterhood of support.

Learn more about this organization, and discover more about organizations and faith communities in your area doing the work of advocacy, affirmation, empowerment, and training with women. Connect. Learn. Give. Grow.[24]

---

[24] https://thistlefarms.org/pages/our-mission

FIVE

Susanna and Salome

Leading from the Margins

Luke 8:1–3 and John 8:1–11

HERSTORY

*Soon afterwards he went on through cities and villages, proclaiming
and bringing the good news of the kingdom of God. The twelve were
with him, as well as some women who had been cured of evil spirits
and infirmities: Mary, called Magdalene, from whom seven demons
had gone out, and Joanna, the wife of Herod's steward Chuza,
and Susanna, and many others, who provided for them
out of their resources.*[25]

***

*And Jesus went to the Mount of Olives. Early in the morning
he came again to the temple. All the people came to him and he
sat down and began to teach them. The scribes and the Pharisees
brought a woman who had been caught in adultery; and making
her stand before all of them, they said to him, "Teacher, this woman
was caught in the very act of committing adultery. Now in the law
Moses commanded us to stone such women. Now what do you say?"
They said this to test him, so that they might have some charge to
bring against him. Jesus bent down and wrote with his finger on
the ground. When they kept on questioning him, he straightened up
and said to them, "Let anyone among you who is without sin be the
first to throw the stone at her." Once again he bent down and wrote*

---

[25] Luke 8:1–3, *New Revised Standard Version.*

*on the ground. When they heard it, they went away, one by one,
beginning with the elders; and Jesus was left alone with
the woman standing before him.*

*Jesus straightened up and said to her, "Woman, where are they?
Has no one condemned you?"*

She said, "No one, sir."

*And Jesus said, "Neither do I condemn you. Go on your way,
and from now on do not sin again."*[26]

* * *

I am an olive tree, crooked, gnarled, and worn under the sun. Alive on a hillside just outside of Jerusalem, I purify dead bodies and survive on very little water. Just because I do not need much water to survive doesn't mean I don't crave it with every fiber of my being. I've been thirsty since the day I was born.

* * *

I am a lily of the valley, sweet and understated, intoxicating creation with my scent. Uncontained and wild. I am not to be consumed.

* * *

Growing up in the courts of privilege and power, we had plenty of water. We had tables set with feasts for days. We enjoyed abundance pouring over and out into our mouths, making its way into our bellies. We wanted for nothing.

Yet, as a little girl, I remember sitting at the window, gazing out at the hills, thinking, *There must be more than this.*

When I was twelve, I was walking through the market when a child around four years of age pulled at the hem of my robe asking for money. My eyes met theirs for a moment, and as I reached into my purse to hand them a coin, I was swept up by one of my father's security guards.

---

[26] John 8:1–11, *New Revised Standard Version.*

Later that night, my mother, having heard of my close encounter with "the poor," scolded me:

"We do not touch them. We do not befriend them. We remain separate. We trust that the government will provide for them as needed."

She said it directly and without feeling. That was the way it was.

Still, I sat at the window and gazed at the horizon, hell-bent on remembering my feelings: confusion, sadness, fear, longing, joy. If I paid attention to these feelings, if I honored them instead of ignored them, might they lead me where I wanted to go?

* * *

In certain translations Susanna means "joy." In others it means "lily of the valley." Both translations seem to call me to something beyond myself. But could it be that my life's purpose is to embody the meaning of my name? Susanna. Perhaps my name calls me not so much beyond as within.

* * *

When Joanna told me about Jesus, I was eager to learn more.

"He does not speak *of* the poor as if he doesn't know them," she said. "Rather, he speaks *with* them, lives *with* them, *is* one of them. We could pool our resources and help him spread the good news for everyone."

Longing to be a part of something different, I joined Joanna and Mary of Magdala one day to hear this Jesus preach. Honestly, it wasn't his words that captivated me; it was his presence. There was a kindness about him. We often mistake kindness for meekness. But Jesus was not meek. Rather, his kindness felt whole—sharp, wise, direct, clear. I'd spent years listening to arrogant men speak, and it was refreshing to listen to one speak with confidence and clarity.

I returned to the palace that night and told my husband, who served on Joanna's husband's staff, that I wanted to support Jesus' ministry. I was nothing but a side note to him, a distraction from the real business of ruling and conquering, conquering and ruling. Like swatting away a fly, he said, "Sure. Whatever you want."

Jesus was still just a name floating around, another nuisance. It wouldn't be until months later that the government would begin to pay attention to Jesus, viewing him as a threat. At this moment, all my husband knew was that he wanted me to be content and to leave him alone.

I'd given him four sons and no daughters, securing my place as bountiful matriarch. With our sons cared for by palace nurses and maids—women who made it possible for me to conceive of working outside the home in the first place—the time was ripe for me to make a change.

We women are strong, and we women are wise. We give birth and nurture the next generations. In times of war and in times of peace, we plot new ways forward. Jesus knew this to be true of women because he was raised by Mary and grew up learning from his sisters. Jesus recognized our powerful presence, and his recognition of our power made him worth following and supporting.

We women often stand on the margins to observe what is needed, and when we see a need, we set up circles of love, place candles in windows, and lead the way forward to meet the needs that present themselves. Therefore the relationships we seek are ones of mutual recognition and mutual aid, relationships that join us in loving the world, relationships of equal and reciprocal power and support. The relationship we formed with Jesus was exactly this.

* * *

Mary, Joanna, and I began to meet weekly to pool our resources and give them to Jesus and his ministry. We were the original benefactors. We dreamed about inviting other women into the fold, of giving them a soft place to land, a hopeful vision of a world in which they could not only survive but also thrive.

Eve and her mother and sisters were some of the first to join us. Then, others followed. We found additional tents for sleeping at night and during the day began to teach other women skills like basket weaving, wood carving, and bread baking. In each town we visited, Jesus would preach and heal; we would find the market and set up shop. Both were essential to sharing the good news. Jesus had Word and Spirit. We had skills and strategy.

* * *

I gave my time and money to Jesus because I resonated with his values and his appreciation of women and our work, our intelligence, and our faithfulness. He was rather unusual and inhabited his maleness somewhat differently than most other men I knew.

Working with Jesus made me question everything I'd been taught about being a man and being a woman. Was there only one way to be? Could the traits traditionally associated with a man not be taken on by a woman and vice versa? Were women always supposed to be meek and mild? Were men always supposed to be loud and domineering?

In our camp, it seemed that each of us contained multitudes, and drawing upon the depths of these layers is what helped us grow and thrive.

Sometimes Mary would preach while Jesus rested. Other times, James and John would tend to the bread baking over the open fire. I counted the money and kept the books. Joanna got the children to sleep some nights, while other nights she stood guard. We led in the ways that made sense for that time and place, trusting one another completely. We were an honest community of faith, believing in something beyond ourselves while knowing the power beyond existed deeply within us.

Our time together wasn't easy, but it also wasn't difficult. Doing what you love, listening to your heart's desire is like this. Even on the most exhausting of days, I went to bed smiling.

* * *

About a month before Jesus was killed, some men threw a young woman before him and accused her of adultery. Her name was Salome, meaning "peace." The men who hurled her at Jesus' feet sought to trap Jesus as they were often trying to do.

"The law of Moses commands us to stone such women," they said.

How, we wondered, would Jesus respond?

We women formed a circle around Salome and Jesus, leading from the margins. We held hands. We swayed. We breathed. We prayed. This was our leadership strategy. This was the way forward.

Jesus knew that he and she were surrounded in love. This was our best defense, our wisest stance.

"You who are without sin, please, cast the first stone."

Jesus spoke these words quietly, yet everyone heard.

Silence covered us like a blanket. Even the birds held their breath.

My eyes were closed. I was praying.

One by one, I imagined the stones falling out of people's hands and onto the dusty ground. One by one, I imagined the sounds of sandaled feet walking away.

Slowly opening my eyes, I saw that only Jesus and Salome remained, encircled by our love.

"Go and sin no more," he said gently. It was as if he was saying it not so much to Salome, weeping on the ground, but to the men walking away, and to all of us who stood as witnesses that day. And to the earth, to the dirt, to our community, to the city and its leaders, to the world.[27]

"Go and sin no more." It was a cry, a plea, a prayer. The situation required no explanation, no detailed account of her or anyone else's suffering, no long confession or contrite purification.

---

[27] Not all biblical scholars understand this passage as Jesus speaking more broadly or communally. Rather, some do not think Jesus would've said to the woman, "Go and sin no more" if she hadn't, in fact, been sinning. They understand this story more as an individual conversation between Jesus and the woman. However, as imagination and interpretation would have it, I, through Susanna's voice and perspective, describe it and imagine it differently. My intent is to invite you, dear reader, to consider, "What if Jesus was speaking to all of us?" How might that broaden our understanding of sin and the healing needed for our community and our world? It's not that I think Salome was perfect (who of us is?); rather, it's that I think Christianity as we know it has spent too much time focusing on individual blame instead of on collective repentance and communal reconciliation and would benefit greatly if the emphasis were shifted to widen the lens of love.

In those sacred moments, Jesus was asking all of us to sin no more. Not for the sake of personal cleansing but for the sake of an unjust world, a world more interested in shaming women than in feeding them.

I heard Jesus scribble something in the dirt.

As our circle disbanded, Mary took Salome's hand and walked with her back to camp. She was one of ours now. Safe. Held. Loved.

Jesus took the hands of Peter and John.

I stayed back for a few minutes, trying to catch my breath.

When I looked at the ground where Salome had fallen, where Jesus had knelt and written in the dirt, where we encircled her, where self-righteous men had walked away, I saw what Jesus had written: *Go and sin no more.*

He both wrote it and said it, prayed it and cried it, sang it and lived it. His words weren't for Salome, at least not solely. Written there in the brown dirt was confirmation that his words were for all of us.

* * *

Into this brown dirt, I was rooted, planted, consecrated. Both an olive tree and a lily, both rough and soft, singular and prolific, I was a disciple of Jesus, a learner, a follower, a leader, a funder. And I was also a witness—to brokenness and blessing, to heartbreak and heart repair, to sin and salvation.

Containing multitudes of both joy and sorrow, I like to believe an olive tree still stands on the hillside where Jesus died, providing shade and purification for the bodies buried there. I like to believe that somewhere in a valley encircled by mountains of love, lilies grow fragrant and uncontainable, wild among the fields. And that a young woman of about sixteen might rest under my branches or lie down in the fields where I grow, hearing an ancient call of repentance, trusting an age-old song of joy, knowing the power of Jesus, the women who encircled and funded him, and their community of love.

LITURGY FOR NIGHT PRAYER

OPENING

If you are gathered with others, position yourselves in a circle. Place a candle in the center. If you are alone, light a candle as a sign of connection to the circle of women saints who join you, even now, as you pray.

Beginning Prayer

Into our most vulnerable God's hands we give this night.[28]
Amen.

With gratitude and longing, joy and sorrow, vulnerability and uncertainty, we sit in the dark with our God. **Amen.**

With praise and thanksgiving, fear and trepidation, wonder and weariness, we offer this day and all its holdings to God. **Amen.**

From sunrise to sunset, our lives rest in the heart of our God. **Amen.**

Prayer of Confession

Find a rock or stone to hold while praying. Holding the stone or rock in the palm of your hand, take your other hand and place it over the stone so it touches the center of both palms. Your hands are in prayer position, cradling the stone as you take the time and space needed to confess what needs confessing, to release what needs releasing.

As you breathe and hold the stone, ask yourself:

What stones do I hold and want to throw?

What might it look like to lay them down?

What is needed to release them to the earth? To let go of my desire for retribution?

What might forgiveness feel like?

After holding several minutes of quiet for reflection and examination, pray this prayer:

---

[28] Richard Rohr in a conversation with Brené Brown: https://brenebrown. com/podcast/spirituality-certitude-and-infinite-love-part-1-of-2/.

God who knows the stones both turned and unturned, both thrown and withheld,

I confess that

I am holding on too tightly,

I want to throw too many,

I am tethered to my anger,

I am bound to my fear.

In the name of Jesus, I repent, release, walk away.

In the spirit of Susanna and Salome, I reconcile, lead, and love.

In the company of all the saints, I ask forgiveness.

Deliver me from shame. Restore me to joy. Help me rest in peace.

Pause for silence.

Amen.

PSALM 13 (inspired by the Common English Bible translation.)

Releasing the stone from your palms, now place it in front of you. Let it rest.

How long will I feel forgotten?

How long will I struggle to see Your face?

How long will I be left to my own devices?

How long will my heart suffer?

Daily? Forever?

Look at me!

Answer me!

I long to be seen and known by You, my God.

I am no longer alive yet dead.

I no longer want the stones I carry to hold power over me,

to steal my joy, to rule my waking and sleeping, to govern my life.

I want to live in peace.

Your faithful love will save me.

My heart will come alive when I sing.

With You, I lay down the stones of bitterness,

And I feast on Your eternal goodness.

Amen.

Scripture Reading: Luke 8:1–3 and John 8:1–11

The Word of Life.

Thanks be to God.

Response

I will go and sin no more.

For the sake of the women

and the world.

For love to grow.

For freedom to multiply.

For healing to manifest.

When I sin, both knowing and not knowing,

I will find You here, every night, holding me in Love.

My spirit and my body, my mind and my heart,

Resting in You.

Song of Praise

"Blessed Is She"

Words and music by Claire K. McKeever-Burgett

The following song can be sung several times through in the practice of meditative singing, the repetition of which offers a deeper connection to God and to the women who are to be followed and whose stories are to be believed.

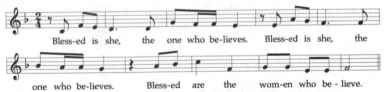

Bless-ed is she,   the   one who be-lieves.   Bless-ed is she,   the

one who be-lieves.   Bless-ed   are   the   wom-en who be - lieve.

Contemporary Connection

*Take a few moments to watch and listen to "One Voice" by The Wailin'
Jennys.*[29] *Imagine Salome and Susanna singing this song together with
the ever-widening circle of women leading from the margins.*

The Prayer of Mary (inspired by Luke 1:46–55)

O Mother God, we glorify You.

From the depths of our beings, we rejoice in You,

Our Deliverer.

As You show mercy to us, help us show mercy to others.

As You honor our bodies, help us honor all other bodies.

**As You scatter the deceitful and remove tyrants from
their thrones,**

help us work for justice and shalom.

Fill the hungry with good things.

Show us what is enough.

Deliver us from pride into mercy.

Deliver us from evil into love.

For Yours is the birthing room, the power, the
vulnerability,

the glory, and the love,

eternally here, and eternally now.

Amen.

Closing Prayer

I am Yours.

I rest in You.

Being seen by You

gives me peace.

Tonight, I rest.

Tomorrow, I rise.

---

[29] https://www.youtube.com/watch?v=y-24qGCvo7A

Forever held and forgiven, saved and soothed
in Your Love.
Amen.

REFLECTION AND CURIOSITY

The following questions are meant to deepen and expand, invite and beckon thoughtful, compassionate, curious responses to the story and liturgy of Susanna and Salome. Whether playing with these questions on your own or in a group setting, carve out space for journaling, collaging, or painting in response. If engaging in a group discussion, choose one or two questions, at most, to hold at the center of your sacred circle.

1. In what ways does your story connect with Susanna's and/or Salome's stories? What resonates? What draws you in?

2. When reading and praying along with Susanna and Salome, what sensations do you notice in your body?

3. What does it look like and feel like for women to advocate for other women? Recall a time in your life when a woman has advocated for you. Spend some time writing about it.

4. When have you held stones too tightly (old resentments and grievances), and what has helped you to lay them down?

5. What does forgiveness look like and feel like for you?

PUBLIC WITNESS

In *Teach a Woman to Fish: Overcoming Poverty Around the Globe*, author Rita Sharma says, "Give a man a fish, and he eats for a day. Teach a man to fish, and he eats for a lifetime. But teach a woman to fish, and everyone eats for a lifetime,"[30] emphasizing the power and vitality of women's work, presence, and witness in the world, not only for themselves, but for everyone. As Susanna and Salome's

---

[30] Sharma, Ritu. *Teach a Woman to Fish: Overcoming Poverty Around the Globe* (New York: Palgrave Macmillan, New York, 2014).

story illustrates, women become agents of healing and love when they invite other women (and people) into their communities, visions, and work in the world.

Women for Women International supports the most marginalized women to earn and save money, improve health and well-being, influence decisions in their home and community, and connect to networks for support. By using skills, knowledge, and resources, women create sustainable change for themselves, their families, and their communities.

The Armah Institute for Emotional Justice identifies the emotional work we all—white, Black, Brown—must do to dismantle harmful systems and to provide resources to do that work. The Armah Institute treats the emotional as structural, as having a pivotal role in sustaining oppressive systems. The implementation home of Emotional Justice, a framework and roadmap for racial healing, The Armah Institute uses storytelling (contemporary lived experience with historical context of race and gender) as a strategy for structural change.

Learn more about these organizations, and discover more about organizations and faith communities in your area doing the work of advocacy, affirmation, empowerment, and training with women. Connect. Learn. Give. Grow.[31]

---

[31] https://www.womenforwomen.org/ and https://www.theaiej.com/about-aeij

Part Two

Two instances in which my mother spoke life-altering truths to me I will never forget, and I will spend the rest of my life sharing them with others because of their (and her) love.

The first happened on the day I was meeting with the district attorney in my hometown to ensure I had protections from the person stalking me, now that I was home from college. Because the person stalking and harassing me lived in another state, a straightforward restraining order would not work, not to mention how difficult the system makes it for people (the majority of them women) to obtain restraining orders when their abusers/stalkers/harassers do live in the same town. Given that the harassment I was experiencing was mostly via phone and online, I was able to meet with the DA and have provisions put in place so that if this person were to visit my state of residence, and if I called the police for protection, they would see the harasser's name in the system and be able to arrest them. My meeting with the DA was a necessary step in this process.

I was sitting across from my mother in my parents' living room. It was midmorning. My appointment was scheduled for just before noon.

"Claire," she said.

I looked up.

"One of the times he called us, he told us that you and he had sex."

I couldn't breathe. I said nothing.

She continued speaking, "Nothing, *nothing* makes his behavior acceptable or means that you are supposed to live in fear. Your father and I don't care what you did or didn't do. We love you no matter what."

Trying both to breathe and not to cry, I quickly nodded as I locked eyes with Mom before gathering my things and leaving the house.

The meeting with the DA went well; protections were put in place for me so that I didn't have to live in constant fear. I honestly don't remember a whole lot about the meeting. I know it happened, and I am grateful. So much of the experience of being stalked, harassed, humiliated, and abused left me feeling disembodied. It would take me years to fully inhabit my skin again and trust it as my holy home. But I do remember the words my mother spoke to me. They were blessing; they were balm; they were freedom.

I grew up in a religious environment in which "True Love Waits" was the slogan for a purity culture in which bodies and their desires for sexual pleasure were not only bad but sinful. In fact, a male Sunday school teacher handed me the book *I Kissed Dating Goodbye* when I was sixteen and encouraged me to read it and practice its truths. And the sex education I received was nothing more than "Don't do it." Therefore, being loved no matter what by my parents after they learned that I had had sex outside of marriage saved me. Once I knew they loved me no matter what, *I* could begin to love me no matter what.

Love not only saved me, it also radicalized me—if being radical means loving without condition, unearthing and retelling stories that center the marginalized, and worshiping at the feet of Mary and of Jesus. Little did my mother realize the spark she was lighting, the force she was awakening. Love is what gave me back to myself and to the women who came before me.

* * *

The second life-altering truth my mother spoke to me was when I was in a long-term relationship in my mid-twenties with someone I would've married in a heartbeat had he asked. We were perfect for each other on paper. But in the actual skin and blood and bone of it, we were a disaster. He activated every insecurity I'd ever known (and even some I was just beginning to know), and I imagine I did the same for him. This was the first relationship in which I learned that love is not enough. Though we loved each other deeply, we didn't need to be together long-term. Holding these two truths with curiosity, compassion, and kindness ultimately became my invitation into deeper healing. But whoever said healing didn't hurt like hell was lying.

We were home for my parents' thirtieth wedding anniversary. My boyfriend and his dog were taking a nap in another room. I was with my mom in the office/guest bedroom.

"Claire." She said my name like a sentence. My head jerked up, and I looked her in the eyes.

"You don't have to do this if you don't want to," she said.

"What are you talking about?" I laughed nervously.

"Your relationship. With him. It doesn't have to be this hard."

My jaw clenched. My shoulders tensed. My eyes looked away ever so slightly as they always did when faced with a truth I didn't want to admit.

"We're fine, Mom," I said. "We will make this work."

"Okay," she replied with a sigh. "It *can* be easy. Life is hard enough as it is. Your relationship doesn't have to be."

I'm sure I rolled my eyes, my first and surefire line of defense against vulnerability, and then I left the room.

It would be another seven months before the relationship came to an end, with him being the brave one to walk away (something for which I will always give him credit and gratitude). I was too lost even to begin to know what making a healthy, brave decision could look like. It would take many months longer to remember my mother's words with wonder and gratitude.

Yet remember I did, and I still do. *It can be easy.*

* * *

Twelve months later, at the ripe young age of twenty-six, I stepped foot onto Vanderbilt University's campus to enroll in its divinity school. I arrived in Nashville fresh out of a heartbreaking relationship, eager for a change of scenery and life, and the divinity school offered me a thought-provoking place to land.

We were sitting in the dean's office for a new-student get-to-know-you session in the fall of our first year as divinity school students. Adam—unbeknownst to me then my future life partner and love—was one of the other new students. He had long sideburns, a soul patch, clear blue eyes, and an easy presence. I immediately wrote him off as "one of the nice white guys who is married" and didn't think about him again until our mutual friend invited him to join us for pizza and beer on a random Tuesday in March.

Turns out he wasn't married after all, and the same easy presence I recalled from the dean's office was still present over dinner and drinks. In an attempt at playfulness, I asked him if he wanted to get married upon hearing that he, like me, did not care for camping and loved the HBO television series *The Wire*.

He blushed. I laughed. It was the start of something wonderful.

As our relationship progressed, I remember trying to find the words to tell him, "I've been stalked," and "I don't think having sex before marriage is wrong." While this may seem trivial to the more sexually liberated among us, it felt big and important to me, given my conservative upbringing and past. I was still fumbling through, trying to make sense of my story, trying to find my feet and legs beneath me, trying to stand on my own solid, sacred ground.

I was still learning a sexual ethic of liberation and pleasure (a lifelong journey), and trying to remember that sexuality is a gift, not a liability, and that consent, reciprocity, and mutuality are essential pieces of any intimate relationship, especially the relationship I have with myself.

Was it any wonder that my hands were sweaty and my heart was racing as I stood before someone I loved, ready to lay bare what I knew to be most true and right and good?

"I'm a survivor of emotional abuse and stalking," I said. "Sometimes I still worry that he'll show up unannounced either online or at my doorstep to torture and humiliate me."

Hot tears grew behind my eyes. I took a deep breath and continued.

"I've also had sex with other people, and I don't think I'm wrong because of it. I refuse to wear this as a scarlet letter. I refuse to let this define me or keep me afraid. I refuse to let this keep me from love."

It was quiet for a long time. We were worshippers at the altar of honesty and love.

"I hear you, and I see you," he said.

His crystal-blue eyes stared into mine. "I'm here with you, all of you. I'm not going anywhere."

While what he said felt comforting and affirming, it's what he didn't say that made the difference.

There was no, "I forgive you" or "We've all made mistakes" or "I will look beyond your past," as if he believed I'd done something wrong that needed his forgiveness or pardon. Instead, what he said by *not* saying those things was that he wanted to be with me—*all of me*—without the baggage of shame and guilt that a patriarchal religious system steeped in misogyny would have us carry.

With ease, we unpacked that bag, laid it down, and walked away, hand in hand, toward a horizon inviting us to be open, honest, and free.

* * *

We married on a warm, dry day in Napa, California, with a small community of family and friends who celebrated our union with music, prayer, poetry, food, wine, beer, and dancing.

I was clear I was not going to change my name, which then left me with the question, "What name will I have?" It made the most sense to us to combine our names, inviting the lovely yet pesky hyphen into our vernacular. McKeever-Burgett, a sign of connection and compromise, and a very clear signal to our future offspring: you come from us both, so you will bear both of our names. We did it for ourselves, sure, and we did it for our children. Before we knew them, we knew the possibility of them, and the possibility of them was made real because of our love.

Of course, the more I explored the history of naming, the more I learned about the tensions inherent within our names, especially for women. Because even our "family" names are the names of our fathers and their fathers before them, and so on. What would our names be if we had had the power to name ourselves all along?

To name and be named is everything.

* * *

I'd be lying if I said I haven't struggled with the concept of ease throughout my adult life, particularly as I've become more and more aware of my privilege as a socially constructed white, heterosexual woman. When the world is so hard for so many, why do I get to choose ease? And isn't the ability to choose ease also steeped in privilege?

Upon deeper exploration, I've come to understand that my mom was not saying that everything *should* be easy or that everything is equally easy for all of us; she was simply saying that in our closest, most intimate relationships, we can aim for ease, peace, and wholeness between us because life will be hard no matter who we are. Heartbreak and grief are part of the human experience, and it's really beautiful to have someone by your side (and in your bed and bank account and birthing room) who will join you in the anguish and come alongside you as you heal from it.

Mom, I imagine, had learned the truths she spoke to me, over me, and into me through her own heartbreak and grief. God knows that I spend my days giving thanks that she not only learned them but also chose to share them with me. That she found her voice and used it. That she found her healing and shared it, woman to woman, mother to daughter. Isn't that how it has always been and will always be? By sharing some of her story with me, my mother invited me into a love that healed me—and still heals me.

Healing is a curve,

a loop, a cylinder,

a spiraling down.

A ride through the clouds.

A long, slow walk through the desert.

It is everything (and more)

in between.

Healing is lifelong,

layer by layer.

Never a series of problems to solve.

Always a collection of stories, experiences,

people to love.

May gentleness, kindness, patience, joy

be yours for the journey.

You are magnificent

and worth every hard-earned step

it takes.

Get free. Shed the lies.

Dance in the rain. Sleep under the moon.

Eat what your body tells you it wants.

Listen. Listen. Listen.

Mother Wisdom is inside of you,

whispering sweet everythings in your ear

as if your very life depends on it.

Six

Adama

Daughter, Your Blood Has Healed You
Luke 8:43–48

HERSTORY

A woman was there who had been bleeding for twelve years. She had spent her entire livelihood on doctors, but no one could heal her. She came up behind him and touched the hem of his clothes, and at once her bleeding stopped.[32]

My name is Adama, meaning "earth" or "soil" in Hebrew.

Is a name given or chosen? Perhaps it is both.

When I started bleeding at the age of eleven, it was as if my name and its meaning were mocking me—the blood from my uterus so much like the brown of my earthen name. The two connected and unwilling to leave me. My name, a harbinger of the life to come.

Because when I started bleeding, it never stopped. It became my constant companion, a reminder not of my power, but of my liability; not of my beauty, but of my disgrace.

The women in my family and village were used to going to the Red Tent[33] each month when they started bleeding. For many,

---

[32] Luke 8:43–44, *Common English Bible.*

[33] There are differences of thought regarding the "Red Tent" and whether Adama and other women in her family and community would've gone there when they bled. In this story, I operate with the understanding that women's bleeding was considered unclean by the religious culture in which they lived; therefore when they bled, they were required to remove themselves from the places and people of everyday life until the bleeding was complete. I also take liberties to reframe the Red Tent as a place of women's empowerment, celebration, and love rather than a place of banishment and exile.

it was a reprieve from living in a man's world. For as long as their menstruation lasted, the only interactions were with other women, and it was glorious—a haven from the expectations to manage not only their lives, but of the lives of their husbands, sons, and fathers.

In the Red Tent there was laughter and crying, dancing and poetry. The bleeding was understood as power, evidence that life was welcome. (Of course, this was the understanding for the women whose bleeding stopped when it was supposed to stop.)

At first, when my mother didn't know what to do with me, I stayed in the Red Tent. The midwives looked after me in between their other patients. They fed me herbs, gave me lavender to breathe, exercises to try. After a year of what became known as "chronic menstruation," I was given a "room" in the back of the barn. It was more of an open-air corner near the barn animals. This became my dwelling place, and I was grateful my father didn't send me to the streets as was the common practice for girls who didn't stop bleeding. He showed me mercy.

As the years progressed, my mother convinced my father to send me to doctors in other villages, none of whom could help me, all of whom gladly took our money and ran. Because of my blood, I could not marry, I could not worship with others, I could not join the family table. Because of my blood, I was relegated to a life alone, save the times my mother would visit and with tears in her eyes say, "I'm so sorry I can't take this from you."

You are not God, I would think.

Of course, if God could take this from me, what kind of God would that be? A malicious one who had the power to heal but simply wouldn't?

If this were the case, I wanted nothing to do with this God.

* * *

Every month, I was allowed to shop on the outskirts of our village, accompanied by my niece. I would eye the vegetables or oils I needed and send her into the crowds to buy them. Technically, this was not allowed, seeing as constant bleeding made me—and therefore anyone with whom I interacted—"unclean."[34] However, our village was small, and people had pity on me, on my family.

It always struck me as odd that the blood from the very place that created life was understood as "unclean." It also struck me as incongruent that somehow my uncleanliness affected everyone else. Yet I dared not question. I was lucky to be alive, though with malady.[35]

On the day I touched the hem of his garment, I was exhausted. Bleeding for twelve years with no reprieve left me depleted and haggard. The brush of my hand at the foot of his robe was an accident, or perhaps it is more accurate to say that it was motivated by something other than me. I was either so deeply in my body that I was unconscious of my next move, or I was so ethereally outside of my body that I didn't have control over what came next. Either way—and maybe both ways—my hand would not stop itself from reaching toward him.

I did not think, *He will save me. He is the answer to all my problems. His skin will relieve my skin of its stain.* For I'd long given up on a Savior.

However, I do remember being intrigued by his presence, drawn in by his tone. Desperate for some relief of the bleeding—and even more desperate for a God who not only cared about my blood but also celebrated it, blessed it, and honored it—I sensed some inkling of this kind of God living in Jesus.

The crowds were thick, and instead of staying back as I was told to do, I joined the crowd, touching shoulders and bodies with others, pretending this was allowed. Fortunately, the throngs of people clamoring for his attention distracted from my illicit presence there. I only meant to follow, to listen, to investigate. But when he stopped suddenly and without warning, it caused a ripple effect among the

---

[34] Not all biblical scholars agree that Adama would have been excluded from her family or community based on her condition. However, my understanding is that constant bleeding was socially debilitating, which caused isolation or, at the very least, disconnection from her community.

[35] Again, not all biblical scholars agree that Adama would've been considered unclean. However, I use "unclean" here based on the translation of the biblical text from which I read this story and to challenge the idea of blood as impure or unclean in the first place, hence the use of quotation marks around the word.

people. I tripped over the person in front of me, falling forward, landing at Jesus' feet.

Anyone in their right mind, especially given my condition, would have crawled away as quickly and quietly as possible. After all, I was not supposed to be there, much less be encountering others.

But something overcame me, and instead of slinking away, I looked down at the red earth from which I had garnered my name and began to caress it like it was my child. Moving my hand back and forth, back and forth, I blessed the earth, and in blessing it, I began to bless myself.

The back-and-forth motion of my hand is what brought me to the hem of his garment. The blessing of God's earthen body became the blessing of my own. For as I skimmed his cloak, my bleeding ceased.

I knew at once that I'd been healed. Jerking my head up, startled, I looked around only to lock eyes with Jesus.

He didn't say anything at first, only walked toward me—*Adama, earth daughter*. Looking me in the eye, he asked, "Did you touch my cloak?" Unable to speak, I nodded yes.

What came out of his mouth and heart next is what preachers and theologians have been quoting for centuries: "Daughter, your faith has healed you."

To this day, I'm not convinced he knew that he'd just healed me of a lifetime of bleeding. All he knew was what we both felt— an exchange, a sharing of power. With one simple, unconscious, uncontrollable touch, I stopped bleeding, something I would never fully understand but would gratefully honor for the rest of my days.

That's the thing with miracles: they're not meant to be understood, parsed out, detailed, and excavated. At their purest invitation, they say, "Come, join me in the mystery. Accept me for what I am—pure, unadulterated grace."

Jesus was generous to say that it was my faith that healed me that day. For it always felt to me that it was the brown earth, the blood of my body, that healed me. The blood, the very thing from which I needed healing, became the salve, the remedy, my redemption.

My name is Adama: earth daughter, healing and healed.

LITURGY FOR MORNING PRAYER

OPENING

If you are gathered with others or alone, consider practicing this liturgy as you walk outside or sit on the porch or lie in the grass. Allow the sun or the moon to serve in place of your candle. If outside space is not accessible to you, find a comfortable place to sit as close to the ground or floor as comfortably possible.

Opening Earth Proclamation

The earth is among us and within us.

May the earth, the ground of our being, lead us wherever we go.

Thanks be to God!

Amen.

Opening Prayer

You, O God, are our ground, our foundation, our support.

From You we come; to You we shall return.

From sunrise to sunset, from dark skies to colored dawns,

From dry plains to drenched valleys, from mountains to seas,

May we rest in Your healing and find peace in Your love,

Trusting that when we tend to our own healing, we tend to others' healing as well. Amen.

Psalm 24:1–6 (inspired by the Common English Bible translation)

The earth is in God. God is in the earth.

All who live within the earth are a part of God,

And God is a part of them.

From seas to rivers, God is alive.

Who will open their eyes to see God everywhere?

Who will stand, feet on the ground,
Knowing in Holy God they stand?
Those who dig their hands into the earth,
Those who are unafraid to get dirty,
Those who acknowledge life within them,
Those who are unafraid of blood,
Those who seek the healing
of the God of Leah, Rachel, Hagar, Tamar, and Miriam
Will receive blessing upon blessing,
Healing upon healing
from the God who saves.

Scripture Reading: Luke 8:43–48
A life-giving Word.
Thanks be to God.
Silence

Prayers from the Earth and Its People
Mother Earth,
Gather all your people together,
Make a circle around us.
Help us listen to the wisdom of the mountains,
The peace of the rivers,
The kindness of the forests,
The love of the oceans.
You know our pain and our heartbreak.
Here may follow prayers, spoken both aloud and in the quiet of our hearts,
for those people and places throughout the world who are in pain and
heartbreak.

Mother Earth,
Gather all your people together,
Make a circle around us.

Help us feel the wisdom of the mountains,

The peace of rivers,

The kindness of forests,

The love of oceans.

You know our joy and our celebration.

Here may follow prayers, spoken both aloud and in the quiet of our hearts, for those people and places throughout the world who know joy and celebration.

Mother Earth,

Gather all your people together,

Make a circle around us.

Help us see the wisdom of the mountains,

The peace of rivers

The kindness of forests

The love of oceans.

You know our pain and our heartbreak,

Our joy and our celebration.

You are with us in and through it all.

Here we are, Mother Earth,

Kneeling at your verdant altar,

Praying, pleading, breaking, being.

Heal us. Make us whole.

Amen.

Song of Praise

"Blessed Is She"
Words and music by Claire K. McKeever-Burgett

The following song can be sung several times through in the practice of meditative singing, the repetition of which offers a deeper connection to God and to the women who are to be followed and whose stories are to be believed.

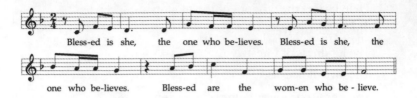

Bless-ed is she, the one who be-lieves. Bless-ed is she, the one who be-lieves. Bless-ed are the wom-en who be - lieve.

Contemporary Connection

Take a few moments to listen to "I Am Perfect as I Am" by A Beautiful Chorus.[36] Imagine Adama singing this song to herself every morning, midday, and night. Imagine singing this song to yourself.

The Prayer of Mary (inspired by Luke 1:46–55)

O Mother God, we glorify You.

From the depths of our beings, we rejoice in You,

Our Deliverer.

As You show mercy to us, help us show mercy to others.

As You honor our bodies, help us honor all other bodies.

As You scatter the deceitful and remove tyrants from their thrones,

help us work for justice and shalom.

Fill the hungry with good things.

Show us what is enough.

Deliver us from pride into mercy.

Deliver us from evil into love.

For Yours is the birthing room, the power, the vulnerability,

the glory, and the love,

eternally here, eternally now.

Amen.

---

[36] https://www.youtube.com/watch?v=dxj3C4Ati0I

Closing Blessing

Children of Mother Earth—

May you be as rooted as the trees,

Free as the birds,

Open as the skies,

Honest as the leaves,

Kind as the daisies

May you bask in the golden

Light of this hour.

May you be healed.

Amen.

REFLECTION AND CURIOSITY

The following questions are meant to deepen and expand, invite and beckon thoughtful, compassionate, curious responses to the story and liturgy of Adama. Whether playing with these questions on your own or in a group setting, carve out space for journaling, collaging, or painting in response. If engaging in a group discussion, choose one or two questions, at most, to hold at the center of your sacred circle.

1. In what ways does your story connect with Adama's? What resonates with you? What draws you in?

2. When reading and praying along with Adama, what sensations do you notice in your body?

3. What did you learn as a child about women and their bleeding? What do you know about it now? What practices might help destigmatize women's bleeding?

4. What is a miracle to you?

PUBLIC WITNESS

Given the culture in which I grew up, I did not learn the beauty and power of my body and its monthly cycle of bleeding and releasing until I was well into my thirties. I was taught to fear the blood of my monthly period. I was taught to hide it, just like I was taught to hide and ignore my sexuality.

As I awakened to my own monthly rhythm and began to interrogate the visceral reactions I often had to it, I began to learn that I need not always love it in order to respect it. I also learned that there were women in the world who did not have access to period products and still lived in societies that shunned them for bleeding, even though this very blood is what enables their societies to continue.

What happened with Adama, the woman who bleeds and does not die, still happens with women throughout the world. Girls and young women continue to feel ashamed of their bodies because others shame them for their bodies' natural, powerful cycles and potentials.

Thankfully, the organizations below are working to correct these ills and empower women, girls, and people with the resources they need to live shame-free, embodied, period- and sex- positive lives.

Bloody Good Period fights for menstrual equity and the rights of all people who bleed by giving period products to those who can't afford them and providing menstrual education to those less likely to access it. They also help everybody talk about periods.

Sex Positive Families provides education and resources that help families raise sexually healthy children using a shame-free, comprehensive, and pleasure-positive approach.

PERIOD. is a global youth fueled nonprofit which strives to eradicate period poverty and stigma through advocacy, education, and service.

Learn more about these organizations, and discover more about organizations and faith communities in your area, doing the work of advocacy, affirmation, empowerment, and education with women, girls, and all who bleed. Connect. Learn. Give. Grow.[37]

---

[37] https://www.bloodygoodperiod.com/, https://sexpositivefamilies.com/about/, and https://period.org/who-we-are

SEVEN

Miriam and Mari

I Am Here
Luke 8:40–42, 49–56

HERSTORY

When Jesus returned, the crowd welcomed him, for they had been waiting for him. A man named Jairus, who was a synagogue leader, came and fell at Jesus' feet. He pleaded with Jesus to come to his house because his only daughter, a twelve-year-old, was dying.[38]

Taking her hand, Jesus called out, "Child, get up." Her life returned and she got up at once. He directed them to give her something to eat. Her parents were beside themselves with joy.[39]

* * *

I never wanted to be a mother, and I wouldn't have been one had I felt I had a choice. I never knew my own mother; she was gone before I turned two.

They say she left. I have no idea where she went. Perhaps she needed a freedom she knew she could never get by staying here. I hope that wherever she is, she is free.

I hid my pregnancy from your father and his family for a long time. Only my sister knew the truth. Even back then I had a sense that there'd be no hiding this from you. Because there you were—inside of me—absorbing my pain and my joy (when I could find it), and

---

[38] Luke 8:40–42, *Common English Bible.*
[39] Luke 8:54–56, *Common English Bible.*

81

there was nothing I could do but live with you right there inside of me and pray that you and I would be okay.

When it came time to bring you to the earth, I climbed into a cave situated high on a hill and screamed you into being. My sister and a midwife were with me. I bled for days afterward. I thought it'd never end.

We named you Mari—close to my own name, Miriam. Scholars of linguistics contest the meaning of our names. But can't we be both beloved and bitter?

Though I never wanted to be a mother, I cared for you thoughtfully and with love, feeding you from my breast, rocking you to sleep. During those first three years, you were attached to me like an appendage. I crawled into you or you crawled into me. Either way, we were inseparable.

I worked not to be listless and disengaged, not to embody the bitterness of my name. The freest from bitterness I felt was when we'd take a blanket to the hillside, spread it wide, and lie in the sun. You weren't so much still as you were active, crawling all over me, working hard to attain the nickname "wiggle worm."

"I love you, my wiggle worm," I'd say as I wiped your snotty nose with the corner of the blanket.

"I wuv you, my iggle urhm," you'd say in return.

I'm remembering you now as a snotty nosed two-year-old as I stare at your limp, sick, twelve-year-old body lying on stained bed linens that we're all terrified to touch lest we disturb you—from what, we do not know.

Even though I never wanted to be a mother, I've been glad to be yours. Now my breath catches at the thought of losing you. I agonize about how someone must do something to help you, how powerless I feel that I can't be the one to do so, how unfair it is that you're so sick.

Flashes of memory interrupt my feelings of agony and powerlessness—of you at age five, throwing perfectly good, freshly baked bread out of the window. Of you at age ten, refusing to eat for two whole weeks. Of how difficult it was to get you to latch onto my breast when you were born, me with my jaw clenched, determined to get you fed, to keep you alive. I remember it being a battle of wills until you gave in and ate.

I hear your father packing a bag, readying himself to leave. There is a holy man he must find. "The holy man will help," he says.

"Go," I say. "Go. I will be here."

Slowly, we lift you from the bed, and as the housemaids change the soiled linens, I take a warm washcloth to your frail body and begin to move it slowly up and down your back, your arms, your face, your legs.

"I am here," I say repeatedly, as if saying it is the remedy.

"I am here."

We lay you back down on the bed. I lie down beside you. Your eyes are closed, but I investigate them nonetheless and see your broken heart.

Were you born with a broken heart? Was it because you knew I never wanted you? Is it enough to want you now? Does every mother fear that their children's problems are their fault? Does every mother live with worry and regret, fear and doubt?

"Only the good ones," I can hear my sister say.

But what even is good?

I run my hand across your forehead and through your hair.

I am here. I am here.

My issues with motherhood weren't only due to the fact that my mother left when I was two; they were also borne of the ought-ness of it, the "this is what women do" of it, the forced labor of motherhood and being a wife with no recognition and very little power, the reality that society would collapse without us and yet there was such little regard for women apart from what we could do, who we could birth. I felt conflicted and confused without anywhere to work out my conflict and confusion. I felt alone and afraid without anywhere to speak of my loneliness and fear.

Every person's story is different, nuanced, and complex in its own unique ways, so I speak for myself and not for all women when I say that feeling forced into a role I didn't want to choose felt like a form of violence. The way I saw it was that men got to design the whole world, assuming that women would do the work of keeping it spinning, leaving us no choice but to buy into their design hook, line, and sinker, or to question it so fiercely that we get ourselves killed or drive ourselves crazy.

I'm somewhere in the middle. Keeping it spinning, questioning it fiercely, and slowly but surely going mad.

You lying here dying compounds all of it. Do you know the faults of this world? Do you know the pain too deeply? Is this why you refuse to eat? Have you known since you were an infant that your refusal to participate in systems of death is what might save you?

When your father returns, there are four men with him. They excuse everyone from the room except for me. You and I are the only women who remain.

"They said she died," your father whispers. "Is she dead? Tell me! Is she dead?"

"I don't know," I say quietly. "I don't know."

Jesus, the holy man whom your father sought out, kneels beside your bed. I do not move from beside you. I am holding on for dear life. Jesus is closer to me than any man has been in a very long time. The unconventionality of it is oddly healing.

"She is only sleeping," Jesus says.

Your father laughs. I sit up on the side of the bed, startled and alert.

He takes one of your hands and places it in mine.

Speaking aloud our names as if they are prayers, he says, "Mari, Miriam! Get up!"

It was as if hearing our names spoken aloud is all we needed. It was as if the clouds parted and the sun started to shine. It was as if he saved not only you, but me too.

At once, you open your eyes and look at me.

"I am here," I say, without saying the words at all.

"Give her something to eat," Jesus says.

I am so disoriented that I almost take off my robe to feed you from my breast. Are you two or twelve?

Before I can move, Jesus hands me a loaf of bread.

"Feed her," he insists.

Hands shaking, I tear a piece from the loaf and hand it to you.

Take. Eat.

Palm open, you receive the bread and lift it to your dry mouth. You eat the bread, then ask for more.

I reach for a basin of water, dip my fingers into its pool, and touch your lips, tracing them with the cool water.

Take. Drink.

We practice the ritual of eating and drinking for what feels like hours. It seems as if you've been reborn, and we are getting to know each other all over again. Only this time, we are older, showing up in different forms, new bodies. Eating bread and drinking water instead of breast milk.

Jesus and his companions leave. Your father eventually retires to bed. Only you and I remain.

In between bites and sips, I wrap my arms around you and repeat my refrain: "I am here. I am here. I am here."

* * *

Looking back on the story of your healing, I am most interested in the ways Jesus gave us back to each other, how he was a doula of sorts, helping bring both you and me back to life. How he spoke our names and touched our bodies in a room full of men. How he needed no diagnosis or doctrine, only faith.

His spiritual direction to both of us was to get up and to get on with living, knowing that there would be plenty of time for dying another day.

* * *

I never wanted to be a mother, though being yours has felt like a gift. It's a complexity I think about even now in my old age as I watch you snuggling your own two-year-old daughter on a blanket on a hill as the sun shines and the wind blows.

No one can prepare you for the complexity of motherhood, whether you want it or not, whether you choose it or not. There's a sense of breathlessness that covers the whole experience, a lifetime of chasing the breath, longing for it to return, only to realize that part of it is no longer yours but your child's. Then you are left hoping and praying it is enough for the both of you. You are left kneeling at the foot of the bed, completely powerless, unable to protect and control, no matter how hard you've tried, with only the words you've heard God pray over you: "I am here. I am here. I am here."

Mari, even when I am no longer here in flesh and bone, I will be here. I hope you can feel this in the deepest parts of your being. I hope you can remember your hand on mine, mine on yours, and the bread for the eating, water for the drinking, and the life for the living.

Amen.

LITURGY FOR EVENING PRAYER

OPENING

Set a table with bread and water. Light a candle. Breathe. Enter this sacred time with quiet and ease, trusting God among you and within you as you pray, as you eat and drink with the women.

Opening Proclamation

May the bread on this table remind us that eating is holy.

May the water on this table remind us that new life is always possible.

May the light remind us of hope.

May the gathering remind us we are not alone.

Thanks be to God. Amen.

Evening Prayer

> In the quiet of the evening,
>
> as the sun sets and nighttime comes,
>
> we give this day to You, God.
>
> All our accomplishments.
>
> All our failures.
>
> All our thoughts.
>
> All our feelings.
>
> All our desires.
>
> All our heartbreaks—
>
> They are Yours,
>
> entrusted to Your grace
>
> and held by Your love.
>
> This is the day that You gave us;
>
> it is Yours both now and forevermore.
>
> **Amen.**

Psalm 139:7–12 (inspired by the Common English Bible translation)

> Your Loving Presence is everywhere, O God.
>
> **When I soar through the sky,**
>
> **When I climb to the birthing cave,**
>
> **When I hunch over in pain,**
>
> **When I descend into death,**
>
> When I rise on the wings of a hawk,
>
> When I turn my face to the noonday sun,
>
> When I spread a blanket for rest and play,
>
> When I do not want the only option I have,
>
> **When I gasp for air,**
>
> **When I lose all I never wanted,**
>
> **When I weep into the depths of the ocean,**

When I feed others,

Your Loving Presence is there.

You find me. You guide me.

You hold me. You love me.

Even when I say, "Surely, I am abandoned,

Surely, I will be swallowed up by the night,"

You say, "The dark is our friend. We will make our way in the midst. You are not alone."

Silence

Scripture Reading: Luke 8:40–42, 49–56

The Word of life.

Thanks be to God.

A moment of quiet for prayer and reflection.

Prayers with the Women

Before praying with the women, break some bread and eat it. Pour the cup of water and drink it. Trust these simple actions to be embodied prayers of healing and love.

We pray with the women who have no options,

We pray with the women who bury children,

We pray with the women displaced by war,

We pray with the women who have no more tears to weep, no more words to say,

Take. Eat.

Take. Drink.

We pray with the women who lead,

We pray with the women who mother,

We pray with the women who are conflicted and confused,

We pray with the women who are clear and kind,

Take. Eat.

Take. Drink.

We pray with the women we know inside of ourselves,

We pray with the desires of our hearts,

We pray for the conscious heartbreaks and the ones we've yet to see,

We pray for food—both spiritual and physical—to fill our plates and our souls,

Take. Eat.

Take. Drink.

For freedom, for choice, for connection, for life,

For all that we know to pray,

For all that we do not know to pray,

Hear us, O God who commands us,

Take. Eat.

Take. Drink.

Amen.

Song of Praise

"Blessed Is She"
Words and music by Claire K. McKeever-Burgett

The following song can be sung several times through in the practice of meditative singing, the repetition of which offers a deeper connection to God and to the women who are to be followed and whose stories are to be believed.

Bless-ed is she, the one who be-lieves. Bless-ed is she, the one who be-lieves. Bless-ed are the wom-en who be-lieve.

Contemporary Connection

Take a few moments to listen to and watch "You've Got to Move" by Mavis Staples and Levon Helm.[40] As you listen and watch, you may want to dance. If so, then dance! Imagine Mari and Miriam dancing together as this song plays.

The Prayer of Mary (inspired by Luke 1:46–55)

O Mother God, we glorify You.

From the depths of our beings, we rejoice in You,
Our Deliverer.

As You show mercy to us, help us show mercy to others.

As You honor our bodies, help us honor all other bodies.

As You scatter the deceitful and remove tyrants from their thrones,

help us work for justice and shalom.

Fill the hungry with good things.

Show us what is enough.

Deliver us from pride into mercy.

Deliver us from evil into love.

For Yours is the birthing room, the power, the vulnerability,

the glory, and the love,

eternally here, eternally now.

Amen.

Closing Blessing

Your presence is food,

Your love is life,

Your joy is everlasting,

Your being is our birthright.

Go now in the presence, love, joy, and being
of God.

---

[40] https://www.youtube.com/watch?v=RFu9qnI3APo

Go now to take, eat; take, drink
of the abundance of God.
Amen.

REFLECTION AND CURIOSITY

The following questions are meant to deepen and expand, invite and beckon thoughtful, compassionate, curious responses to the story and liturgy of Mari and Miriam. Whether playing with these questions on your own or in a group setting, carve out space for journaling, collaging, or painting in response. If engaging in a group discussion, choose one or two questions, at most, to hold at the center of your sacred circle.

1. In what ways does your story connect with Mari's and Miriam's? What resonates? What draws you in?

2. When reading and praying along with Mari and Miriam, what sensations do you notice in your body?

3. What do you know about reproductive justice? What does it mean to you?

4. In what ways can you bear witness to another's story even when it is different from your own?

5. In what ways do eating and drinking play a significant role in your life? What tables are you setting? What tables do you want to set? Who do you want sitting at your table?

6. What do you want? What are the desires of your heart, mind, body, and spirit? What does the world, your family, your church, and your community want of you? Are the answers to these two questions congruent or misaligned? Spend some time reflecting on why.

PUBLIC WITNESS

Some of the most pastoral things I've ever done are drive a friend to get an abortion, help youth access safe and justice-centered sex education (and condoms), hold a friend's heart and hand while she miscarried, help a friend leave an unhealthy marriage, and connect friends to the mental health care they need. All of these took place outside church buildings where God's Spirit and love are alive and well in the ways we care for one another communally.

Perhaps the greatest lie ever told is that church is required for holiness.

Don't get me wrong. Church can and often does foster all kinds of love and connection and care. I'm simply saying that the traditional ways we've come to understand church (a building with pews and hymnals and a pulpit) isn't a requirement for love, connection, and care to take place, and that to pretend that the organizations named and described below are not acting as church for people is to remain limited and confused about what church really is. Church is a place where love, connection, dignity, and healing are handed out like life jackets on a sinking ship; a place where people circle around and say, "How can I help?" and, when they hear the answer, they say, "Okay, we'll figure it out together."

Healthy and Free Tennessee is a network of agencies, organizations, and individuals working together to promote sexual health and reproductive freedom in the state of Tennessee with an organizational focus on the intersections of racism, the criminal legal system, and reproductive justice. Healthy and Free Tennessee fights to improve access to reproductive health care for marginalized communities. It also fights punitive policies that seek to criminalize reproductive outcomes.

SisterSong is a Southern-based, national membership organization whose purpose is to build an effective network of individuals and organizations to improve institutional policies and systems that affect the reproductive lives of marginalized communities.

Indigenous Women Rising is committed to honoring Native and Indigenous people's inherent right to equitable and culturally safe health options through accessible health education, resources, and advocacy.

Crossroads Community Services compassionately serves families through food equity research, innovation, and distribution partnerships, effectively revolutionizing food pantry services and building nutrition-stable communities.

Learn more about these organizations, and discover more about organizations and faith communities in your area doing the work of advocacy, affirmation, empowerment, and education for women and their families. Connect. Learn. Give. Grow.[41]

---

[41] https://www.healthyandfreetn.org/ and https://www.sistersong.net/mission and https://www.iwrising.org/our-mission and https://ccsdallas.org/

EIGHT

Edith, Rachel, Sarah, and Leah

Embodied Blessing

Matthew 13:54–58

HERSTORY

When he came to his hometown, he taught the people in their synagogue. They were surprised and said, "Where did he get this wisdom? Where did he get the power to work miracles? Isn't he the carpenter's son? Isn't his mother named Mary? Aren't James, Joseph, Simon, and Judas his brothers? And his sisters, aren't they here with us? Where did this man get all this?"[42]

* * *

Our mother taught us that if we could find a piece of cloth, a scrap just long enough for us to stretch our arms to one end and our feet to the other, we could have a place all our own. It would be a place of freedom, she told us. A place of deep breaths and open hearts. A place to practice our prayers instead of only saying them.

Our mother knew what it was like to live in a man's world, wrought with external pain born of internal suffering no one would acknowledge. She knew what it was like to need space from men's fears and religious expectations. She knew the thirst for freedom.

So when our grandmothers threw out the cloth scraps, we gathered what we could, pieced a few of them together, and made ourselves mats upon which to rest and move, stretch and play. Rising

[42] Matthew 13:54–56, *Common English Bible.*

before the sun, we'd make our way to the hillside just east of our village, spread our mats upon the ground, turn toward the promise of the sun, open our arms, and breathe. It wouldn't take long for one of us to smile, leading the way for the rest of us to follow.

We'd take turns leading one another. Sometimes it was Rachel; she always invited us to dance. Other times it'd be me, Edith, and I preferred a more restful practice. What divine grace to begin our days as teenagers moving slowly and intentionally! When Sarah led us, we would hold poses for a solid thirty seconds before moving to the next. Leah's practice always focused on the breath in and out with each movement, providing heightened awareness of our bellies and chests expanding and contracting, readying ourselves to create something beautiful.

The day Jesus stumbled upon our circle, the clouds were pregnant with rain. We were rushing to fit in some form of togetherness and movement before they opened and gave birth, so we didn't notice our gentle observer until we began folding our mats and turning back toward home.

I saw him first and asked, "What are you doing here?"

Softly he replied, "I was curious. I wanted to know what you do together before the sun rises."

Rachel, our eldest sister and fearless leader, walked toward us, unphased by Jesus' presence.

"Good morning, brother. You wanna know what we do here? We dance. We play. We move. Just for ourselves and no one else. Would you like to join us tomorrow?"

"He can't join us!" I exclaimed indignantly. "This is just for us!"

Rachel stopped in her tracks and slowly turned toward me.

"I'd rather him participate with us than sit on the sidelines and observe us. Honestly, he could learn a thing or two from us, so let him come. We'll be his teachers."

The next morning I begrudgingly laid out a mat for my brother. He showed up on time, which made me soften toward him ever so slightly. He then participated fully in Rachel's practice, which invited us to dance freely upon the hillside, moving our arms to and fro, forgetting time and space, listening only to our bodies and what and how and where they wanted to go and do and be.

Witnessing Jesus' movements made me realize how hungry he was for power, leadership, and community led by, for, and with women at the center; how the patriarchal society in which we lived robbed him of his full humanity just like it robbed us; how if we wanted to change the systems in which we lived, making more room and space for feminine understandings of God and the world, we'd need to include men in our circles too.

Throughout our teenage years, Jesus joined us every morning. He heard our cries in the opening circle and our sighs of relief as we closed our eyes. He listened closely to the ways we invited one another to participate and move.

"Never a demand; always an invitation," we told him.

"Our bodies are our leaders. We follow them and what they want and need."

One morning, Rachel announced that Jesus would be leading us. Always the wise one, Rachel knew the power of invitation, of widening the circle of inclusion. I, on the other hand, wanted to remain small, insular, and secluded. Letting Jesus into our world felt risky, and I was afraid.

Though we began each morning's practice in a circle, we'd typically break the circle and spread out among the hillside, facing the leader for the day to engage the practice. But instead of dismantling our circle that morning, Jesus invited us to remain in the round. He then took his place in the middle and invited us to find a comfortable place to sit.

"Connect to the earth. Find some stillness. Allow yourself to breathe and be," Jesus said.

At first, I opened my eyes to look at Jesus and my sisters in the circle. It was hard for me to take him seriously. I was used to following my sisters, not Jesus. I was used to how things were, not yet ready for how they might be.

But no one else's eyes were open; they were attuned and engaged. I was left either to follow their lead or leave.

Settling into the grass, I began to surrender, not so much to Jesus but to my breath. *In and out. In and out.* I repeated these words until I was no longer aware I was saying them. I let myself float among the clouds and sail in the peaceful waters of the sea.

Just as the sun started to peek over the horizon, Jesus invited us to take one more deep breath in and one long exhalation out. *Amen.*

We gathered our mats in silence. Something about the quiet we'd experienced together made us reluctant to break it.

As we walked the path home, though, I placed my hand in the center of Jesus' back and whispered, "Thank you."

He turned to me ever so slightly and said, "Sister. Thank you."

When the time came for Jesus to leave and engage his public ministry, I missed him in our daily practice on the hillside. His presence became a welcome one, an expansion of the circle I had wanted to keep closed and small out of fear and ignorance. Which is why, when he packed his things to leave, Rachel, Leah, Sarah, and I made sure he had his own mat, as well as a few extra to share with his companions.

"Remember," Rachel said, "practice is what will sustain you."

* * *

Jesus arrived back in Nazareth on a hot, sticky day. We heard of his arrival before we saw him. Word travels fast in a small town.

He was preaching provocative things in and out of the synagogue. He was celebrating the poor, communing with women, likening fishermen to religious scribes, and encouraging a reverent return to the religious and cultural system upon which all our lives were built. To say the people were disturbed by Jesus' teachings would be an understatement. His call for us to return, understand, and practice the true origins of our faith scandalized, terrified, and upended much of the halfhearted faith we were practicing. Comfort likes to be comfortable, and people like to resist change and repentance. Thus, the crowds began to question the origins of his power: "Where did this man get this wisdom and these deeds of power? Who is this man who questions and admonishes?"

We heard these questions asked boldly at the market and in the sideline whispers at the temple.

"Is this not the carpenter's son? Isn't his mother called Mary? And are not his brothers James and Joseph and Simon and Judas? And are not all his sisters with us? Where did this man get all this?"

As if we weren't the source of his power, or at least part of it, the villagers discounted us and Jesus altogether.

Late one night, I found Jesus sitting in the lamplight, unable to sleep.

"What do you make of our community questioning you and all of us?" I implored. "Why don't you tell them where your power comes from? Why don't you show them who you really are?"

"Sister. I know where my power comes from," Jesus replied. "My power comes from Mother and you and Rachel and Leah and Sarah. From all those days I joined you on the hillside to pray with our bodies and our breath. My power comes from our father teaching me how to use my hands and make something with them. My power comes even from our brothers, who don't always understand but who follow anyway."

"But why don't you tell them this?" I asked.

"Because ultimately, I don't have to. The power from you and Mother and Father and our siblings is power from God. The One who helps us when the morning dawns; the One who holds us steady when the earth shakes. The One who begs us to be still and know God is God. It's not a power to hurl but a power to share. It's not a power to rule but a power to love. Those who can see will see. Those who can follow will follow."

I was uncertain of his peace and had only ever known for myself the power of which he spoke during our times on the hillside every morning with my sisters. For we knew what it was like to share and to love, to lead and to follow. Our embodied practices of breath and movement taught us (and Jesus too) that we would preach many sermons throughout our lifetimes, yet only a handful of them would ever be in front of a listening crowd. Most of them would take place on hillsides and seashores, in stables and at dinner tables, around washing bins and sewing circles, on birthing stools and at bedsides.

Jesus didn't preach many sermons or perform many miracles during his visit home that summer. He spent time resting, praying, and practicing with us, recharging for the next phase of his journey. When I wanted him to shout and prove, he helped me return to breath and silence. When I wanted him to convict, he taught me compassion.

The morning Jesus left, we found each other on the hillside. The same mats we'd been using for years, tattered and in need of repair, had already been laid out, ready for our bodies to bless them with their weight.

Rachel, Leah, Sarah, our mother, Mary, and a gathering of our daughters and nieces, sons and nephews joined us.

"Who will lead?" I asked.

"We both will," Jesus answered.

Then, taking my hand in his, we reached our arms to the sky, inhaled and exhaled, softly and slowly. Everyone followed our lead. No words were needed, only the movement of our bodies, the rhythm of our breath, the holiness of togetherness—the most powerful source on planet Earth.

If anyone had looked eastward that day, they would've seen a gathering of twenty to thirty women, one man, and a host of children. They might have mistaken it for a worship service or a holy gathering with a holy man at the center. They might even have thought, *Where did this man get all this?* Compelled by their curiosity, they might have moved closer and tried to learn more.

Of course, if they had come closer and learned more, been awake and looked eastward, they would've learned what we—Edith, Rachel, Sarah, and Leah—had taught Jesus all those years ago, something our mother taught us, something her mother taught her. There is no limit to holiness, no boundary for the divine. There are bodies and movements, collaboration and stillness, hillsides and sunrises ready and waiting for us to show up and say, "Yes."

Our mother, Mary, said yes to the divine when she was a young girl. It was a yes that paved the way for her daughters to say yes to the predawn embodied prayer practice that gave our lives depth and meaning, safety and community. A yes that allowed her son to say yes to his sisters and to our God.

I'm not convinced Jesus would be Jesus without the hillside, without the movement, without the prayer, without us. In turn, we would not be who we are without him. That's the beauty of relationship at its best: it's a mutual, reciprocal learning, a joining of hands raised high to the heavens, bodies connected and in sync, a brother learning from a sister, a sister learning from a brother in a world that would rather overpower the wisdom of the feminine than let it lead.

Rachel, Sarah, Leah, and me, Edith—Jesus' sisters, teachers, leaders, friends.

LITURGY FOR MORNING PRAYER

OPENING

For today's liturgy you'll need a yoga mat or a blanket. If possible, find a place outside—in the yard, garden, or on the patio or porch—to engage in prayer. If you are gathered with others, position yourselves in a circle. Place a candle in the center. If you are alone, light a candle as a sign of connection to the circle of women saints who join you, even now, as you pray.

Opening Affirmation

Roll out your mat or blanket. Turn eastward. Plant your feet hip-distance apart. Stand your sacred ground. Reach your arms out to the side, up to the sky, bringing them together into your heart as you breathe gently in and out three or four times.

As you move, say these words:

> Our bodies are good and trustworthy.
>
> We will listen to our bodies.
>
> We will go where our bodies lead.

Opening Prayer

> Thank you for this new day, O God. For the waning darkness and the impending light. For the company of the saints and for nature. For noise and for silence. For breath and for bodies

that lead us. For Your Body, forever delivering us into love.
Thank You for this new day, O God, we pray. Amen.

Psalm 46 (inspired by the Common English Bible translation)

God is our hillside and our centering,

present with us everywhere we go.

Though change can feel scary,

We will recognize and name our fear,

Inviting it to rest.

Amidst the tumult

that our unresolved fears create,

We will seek repair.

Holy is the river that flows,

Inviting us to flow along with it,

Making its way to God, our Home.

When the morning dawns, God helps us.

When nations rage, God's voice softens the earth,

Bids us, "Peace."

Be still, says God. Know me.

I am the soft breeze tickling your skin.

I am the malleable earth beneath your feet.

I am the butterfly, the lark, the thistle, the wren.

I, God of Leah and Rachel,

Edith and Sarah,

Mary and Hagar,

Am with you always.

Scripture Reading: Matthew 13:54–56

A moment of quiet for reflection.

Prayers of the People

Find a place on your mat in which to breathe and pray, holding space for breath and quiet for several minutes. Breathe in through the nose, out through the mouth. As you breathe, specific people or places may come to mind. When they do, continue to breathe, trusting that your breath transports them to the light and love of the holy.

Song of Praise

"Blessed Is She"
Words and music by Claire K. McKeever-Burgett

The following song can be sung several times through in the practice of meditative singing, the repetition of which offers a deeper connection to God and to the women who are to be followed and whose stories are to be believed.

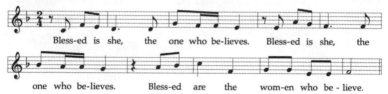

Bless-ed is she, the one who be-lieves. Bless-ed is she, the one who be-lieves. Bless-ed are the wom-en who be-lieve.

Contemporary Connection

Take a few moments to listen to "Light of a Clear Blue Morning," written by Dolly Parton, performed by The Wailin' Jennys.[43] *Imagine Edith, Rachel, Sarah, and Leah singing this together as the sun rises in the east as they unroll their mats and as they pray.*

The Prayer of Mary (inspired by Luke 1:46–55)

O Mother God, we glorify You.

From the depths of our beings, we rejoice in You,

Our Deliverer.

As You show mercy to us, help us show mercy to others.

As You honor our bodies, help us honor all other bodies.

As You scatter the deceitful and remove tyrants from their thrones,

---

[43] https://www.youtube.com/watch?v=J-UK7iNJgNo

help us work for justice and shalom.

Fill the hungry with good things.

Show us what is enough.

Deliver us from pride into mercy.

Deliver us from evil into love.

For Yours is the birthing room, the power, the vulnerability,

the glory, and the love,

eternally here, eternally now.

Amen.

Closing Blessing

Placing one hand on your heart and one on your belly, take three breaths in and out, then speak these words aloud:

God's stillness

God's love

God's breath

God's presence

Be with you.

Be within you.

Be you.

Amen.

REFLECTION AND CURIOSITY

The following questions are meant to deepen and expand, invite and beckon thoughtful, compassionate, curious responses to the story and liturgy of Edith, Rachel, Sarah, and Leah. Whether playing with these questions on your own or in a group setting, carve out space for journaling, collaging, or painting in response. If engaging in a group discussion, choose one or two questions, at most, to hold at the center of your sacred circle.

1. In what ways does your story connect with the stories of Edith, Rachel, Sarah, and Leah? What resonates? What draws you in?

2. When reading and praying along with Edith, Rachel, Sarah, and Leah, what sensations do you notice in your body?

3. In what ways have you experienced the healing power of a community of women or girls?

4. What does mindful, holy movement look like for you?

5. Who have you taught and influenced in your life, whether they've recognized you for it or not?

6. In what ways have you noticed and honored the beauty and power of your body?

PUBLIC WITNESS

I am who I am today in large part because of the people who invited me into embodied spirituality and practice when I was in my twenties and thirties, who introduced me to the practice of yoga, martial arts, and dance, and who taught me that these aren't counter to my faith but a central part of it.

I am a trained practitioner in the Nia technique, which is a movement practice that combines yoga, dance, and martial arts. I am also a trained prenatal and postpartum yoga and barre instructor, as well as a trained birth and postpartum doula. Engaging these sacred movement forms and working primarily with people who identify as women in the space of embodiment and healing, I have learned (and continue to learn) the joy that comes when movement is spontaneous, intuitive, and free.

I've taken the liberty to highlight below two individuals, along with two organizations, whose work empowers women and girls to move as a spiritual practice while honoring the rich cultural and historical traditions from which they come, as well as providing justice-centered approaches to all that they offer.

Homeland Heart understands community health workers as activists and seeks to create a safe space and improve birth outcomes for women, infants, and families of color. Through programming and services designed for women and infants of color, resources for families of color and training and support for women of color midwives and doulas, Homeland Heart Collective is devoted to mitigating concerns and creating safe environments and experiences, eliminating racial, socioeconomic, and health disparities and reducing infant and maternal mortality rates before during and after pregnancy for underserved and marginalized groups.

Act Like a GRRRL is an autobiographical writing and performance program that inspires female-identifying teenagers (ages twelve to eighteen) to write about their lives and transform their thoughts into monologues, dances, and songs for public performance. Act Like a GRRRL is part of the larger Actor's Bridge Ensemble, a nonprofit acting school and professional theater company established in Nashville in 1995 whose mission is to tell the stories Nashville needs to hear as they produce socially conscious plays responsive to the current cultural moment, create new work, train theater artists, and become a safe home for its artists and audiences to find their authentic voices on stage and in life. Actor's Bridge Ensemble is proud to be the leading theater for contemporary works that engage audiences in curiosity and conversation about justice, equity, and inclusion. The company is led by cofounder and producing artistic director Vali Forrister.

Sarah Jane Chapman is a trauma-informed yoga instructor who helps people find a more peaceful home in their minds, bodies, and spirits.

Melissa Shah deeply believes in applying the culture and teachings of yoga to bring to light the long-standing disparities in wellness spaces. She is passionate about bringing yoga and Ayurveda back to its roots.

Learn more about these organizations and individuals, and discover more about organizations, individuals, and faith communities in your area that are doing similar work of embodiment to uplift women, girls, and the divine, sacred feminine. Connect. Learn. Give. Grow.[44]

---

[44] https://www.homelandheart.com/about and https://actorsbridge.org/act-like-a-grrrl/ and https://www.sarahjanechapman.com/ and https://www.findyourbreath.net/

NINE

Ashera and Talliya

"Nasty" Woman

Matthew 15:21–28

Content warning: sexual assault, abuse, rape, mental illness

HERSTORY

*Just then a Canaanite woman from that region came out
and started shouting.*

*Have mercy on me, Lord, Son of David; my daughter is
tormented by a demon.*[45]

Ashera

I was a woman possessed—by my passion, my outrage, and my
desperation.

My daughter, possessed by her pain, pain caused by men and
those who supported them, needed help.

Make no mistake: it takes a whole village of disease to enable
the violence done in the name of a male God. That is why it felt
counterintuitive to approach a man—a holy one at that—about her
healing.

I didn't approach him so much as confront him, demanding of
him to give me something I had to have—my daughter's life and
therefore my own. There was nothing I would not do to save her.

---

[45] Matthew 15:22, *New Revised Standard Version.*

* * *

As was customary, I was married when I turned eighteen. Dagan was ten years my senior and wore his lust for power and domination like a cloak. My parents had no choice but to marry me to him. I was to participate in the sick system of marriage or die. Marriage meant financial security not only for me, but also for my family.

Further, living in conquered lands meant collusion with the empire. This was often the wisest choice if you wanted to survive, and Dagan was nothing if not politically adept at placating the powers that be to survive. "Go along to get along" was his mantra as he schemed to get ahead in city government while holding a fragile peace with surrounding powers.

Dagan's disregard for women was obvious. We were unfit for anything other than bringing him pleasure and offspring. When all was said and done, I birthed him three children, two boys and then a girl. Once he had a girl, he didn't dare risk having another, so our sexual relations ceased, much to my relief.

Since my parents named me Ashera after the Canaanite goddess of earth, I named my daughter Talliya after Ashera's and Baal's daughter in Canaanite mythology, the goddess of rain. I kept Talliya as close to me as I could. While I loved my sons, because they were male all my efforts to protect them from their father's evil ways were fruitless. With Talliya, I felt I had a fighting chance to keep her safe and close, protected from Dagan and his army of male counterparts who did nothing but wreak havoc in the name of male gods they made much more in their own likeness than the other way around.

In the end, I had very little power in Dagan's home. As Talliya came of age, still a child yet growing into a woman, I could not protect her from the men who treated our home like they owned it and all within it. A man only had to let Dagan know he wanted a woman, and Dagan would find one of us for him.

This is how Talliya became "demon possessed." She was raped repeatedly by the men her father called friends. Her pain was too much for her to bear; therefore, she went "crazy." Crazy, according to the townspeople, because the mental emotional burden of wellbeing is always placed upon the woman and not upon the sick society that makes her unwell. Because of her mental illness, Dagan could no longer tolerate us, so he sent us back to my family home where we moved into a small room in the house, grateful to be together and alive.

Still, Talliya suffered from nightmares, loss of appetite, and periodic wailing. I tried to soothe her with lavender and water, canvas and paint. When she'd let me, I would hold her close, rocking her back and forth, back and forth, just as I did when she was a baby, my salty tears finding their way down my cheeks and onto her head as she settled against my heart.

Are these tears enough to save her? I wondered. *Please, God, please let them be the healing she and I both need.*

* * *

I'd heard rumors of a holy Jewish man named Jesus who was traveling along the shore, preaching good news not only to men, but to women and children too. They said he performed miracles, healing the sick and restoring sight to the blind. They said he came for the lost sheep of Israel. I hoped he would, perhaps, come for us too.

If Jesus comes near us, I thought, *I will find him. He will heal my daughter.*

What other choice did I have? Perhaps the most haunting reality of parenting is the fact that you cannot save your children from pain. You can try to prepare them for it; you can be honest with them about it; you can give them the tools they need to confront pain with honesty and compassion. But keeping them from pain is impossible, especially when you show up as a woman in a man's world, as a stranger in an occupied land, as a person without money or status unless a man (your abuser) is there to legitimize you.

Make no mistake, some of us experience much more pain than others. It is a failed system. As a mother, I was determined to do everything I could to make circumstances better for my daughter. If I could alleviate some of her pain, then I might be able to alleviate other women's pain. A slow, steady stream of love birthed from the depths of a woman's healing and a mother's advocacy flowing outward and onward, water for a renewal we women could give to one another.

* * *

Jesus and a gaggle of men were walking through the fish market along the shore. People were following and grasping at his heels. He was solely focused on his destination, trying to ignore the requests hurled his way.

As a woman of considerable size, that day I used the breadth of my body to place myself in the middle of the crowd. Being tall and large, I had a voice that carried, and I used it.

"Have mercy on me, Lord, Son of David. My daughter is tormented by a demon," I shouted.

Jesus ignored me and kept walking. The men traveling with him tried to push me away and implored him, "Send her away, for she keeps shouting after us."

To which Jesus replied, "I was sent only to the lost sheep of Israel." He was rebuffing me, or so it seemed.

So, I thrust my large body in front of Jesus, causing the crowd to stop. Kneeling before him, I pleaded again: "Lord, help me."

I was not expecting a holy man to insult me like he did.

"It's not fair to take the children's food and throw it to the dogs," he retorted.

A dog? Lower than the dogs? *Nasty woman.* This is what I am? A woman begging for her daughter's healing is not worthy of this man's attention, or grace, or understanding? Instead, she is left to insult, injury, and ignorance?

Unyielding, I got to my feet, rolled my shoulders back, and lifted my chin. I looked Jesus directly in the eyes and said, "Yes, Lord, yet even the dogs eat the crumbs that fall from their masters' table."

Sure, I'll be a dog if it means healing for my daughter, bone of my bone, flesh of my flesh. I'll be a nasty woman and wear that label proudly if it means relief might come for us.

Don't you dare use my body and my status as a woman and an outcast against me, I thought. I'll take your insult and turn it into everything that will make you pay attention to my pain, everything that will make you see me, my daughter, and the healing we demand and deserve.

* * *

At that very moment her daughter was healed.[46]

Talliya

I watched my mother confront Jesus. I watched him hurl an insult her way. I watched her get to her feet, look him in the eyes, and persist in her request for my healing.

Witnessing my mother confront this holy man is what healed me. Beholding her belief in me, Talliya, goddess of rain, I watched my mother, Ashera, goddess of the earth, stand in the face of a holy man and demand that he and his holy followers do better and be better.

Her voice opened the heavens. Her body beckoned the dove. Her audacity, like the spirit of the living God, descended upon me, and I was at peace.

We walked to the shore and sank into the salty water. We let it renew us. As the waves made their way in and out, we rocked with their rhythm and sang with their tune.

Later that night, by the light of a small candle, I rolled out the sheepskin, pulled out my paints, and began creating the scene I'd longed for with every shake, nightmare, and wail. It was an ocean of dark blue, purple, and green. White foam danced from large and small waves. A full moon hung low over the sea. I painted a picture of a place where I need not sink nor swim but could simply float. Supported by my mother's love, an ocean of experience poured out of me and onto the canvas, marked by both pain and praise, sorrow and joy.

Mom always said that when she looked at me, it was as if she were looking at herself. It is a strange sensation, she remarked, to see your heart standing, breathing, and existing outside of you. I finally understood what she meant after witnessing her confrontation with Jesus. Because as I watched and listened, I began to see my heart standing before a holy man, too, demanding he pay attention, demanding he see.

---

[46] Matthew 15:28b, *New Revised Standard Version.*

In the end, Mom and I were survivors, rising above, living the only life we knew to live, one inextricably bound to and redeemed by each other.

LITURGY FOR MORNING PRAYER

OPENING

In preparation for this liturgy, gather something from the earth—a stone, some dirt, a blade of grass, a fallen leaf. Have a bowl of water available, then light a candle. Earth represents Ashera; water represents Talliya; and the candle represents the Spirit of God present with us here and now. If you are gathered with others, position yourselves in a circle. Place the candle, your earth offerings, and the bowl of water in the center. If you are alone, place the candle, your earth offerings, and the bowl of water in front of you as a sign of connection to the circle of women saints who join you, even now, as you pray.

Opening Proclamation

> The Spirit of God is among us.
>
> She descends upon us like a dove,
>
> Making peace in our hearts,
>
> Healing our wounds,
>
> Affirming our goodness,
>
> Blessing our bodies.
>
> **Alleluia. Her name be praised!**

Morning Prayer

> Spirit of the earth, sky, water, and fire,
>
> Spirit of every creature and element,
>
> Every person and place,
>
> We give thanks for Your presence among us,
>
> For this new day, which is a gift.

Where we fall short, help us lengthen.

Where we ignore, help us see.

Where we insult, help us repair.

For it is in You and Your Spirit

That we live and move and have our being–

Rocking with the waves,

Resting on the shore,

Baptizing ourselves into new life with You.

Amen.

Psalm 23 (inspired by the *Common English Bible* **translation** and *Psalms for Praying* by Nan C. Merrill)

You are my Shepherd, my guide.

In You, I want for nothing.

You lay me down in soft, singing grass,

Beside melodic waters, I rest.

Here, You restore my soul.

Through constant presence

and abundant love,

You lead me along the path

of my healing.

When I was raped, used, and abused,

Discarded and stolen from myself

By evil men, I was terrified,

Yet You walked with me in my fear.

Your breast, a place to rest.

Your hand, something to hold.

These comforted me.

When I shook and screamed,

You showed me a table of abundance

Where I could dine in the safety and communion
Of women survivors.
When I couldn't sleep,
You offered me oil,
An anointing,
A baptism,
A confession:
You are perfect, holy, and good
Just as you are. Just as you are.
Nothing is certain but Your mercy.
You are my refuge,
forever.
Amen.

Scripture Reading: Matthew 15:21–28
The Word of life.
Thanks be to God.

Prayers of the People

Our prayers this day are "groans too deep for words." So in the tradition of centering prayer, hold five, ten, or twenty minutes of silence as the prayers for the people. The elements of earth, water, and fire may serve as helpful centering points as you hold this space of silent prayer. If you have a bowl of water, you may dip your hands in it. If you have dirt or a stone, it might be a helpful practice to run your fingers through the dirt or to hold the stone as you pray. The fire of the candle can help you focus your attention. If you find your mind drifting, choose a word, and return to it repeatedly. There is no right or wrong way to pray silently. So set a timer, invite God's presence, and hold the quiet space needed for the groans too deep for words to come forth.

Song of Praise

"Blessed Is She"
Words and music by Claire K. McKeever–Burgett

The following song can be sung several times through in the practice of meditative singing, the repetition of which offers a deeper connection to God and to the women who are to be followed and whose stories are to be believed.

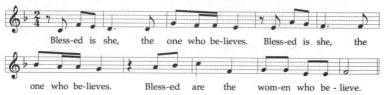

Bless-ed is she, the one who be-lieves. Bless-ed is she, the one who be-lieves. Bless-ed are the wom-en who be - lieve.

Contemporary Connection

Take a few moments to listen to "The 23rd Psalm (Dedicated to My Mother)," written by Bobby McFerrin, performed by Pacific Choral.[47] *Imagine a chorus singing this over and around and among and within Ashera and Talliya while they float peacefully in the ocean together.*

The Prayer of Mary (inspired by Luke 1:46-55)

O Mother God, we glorify You.

From the depths of our beings, we rejoice in You,

Our Deliverer.

As You show mercy to us, help us show mercy to others.

As You honor our bodies, help us honor all other bodies.

As You scatter the deceitful and remove tyrants from their thrones,

help us work for justice and shalom.

Fill the hungry with good things.

Show us what is enough.

Deliver us from pride into mercy.

Deliver us from evil into love.

---

[47] https://www.youtube.com/watch?v=oYTd3Yp3iMg

For Yours is the birthing room, the power, the vulnerability,

the glory, and the love,

eternally here, eternally now.

Amen.

Closing Blessing

Taking the bowl of water, dip your fingers in it, bring them to your forehead, make a circle, and say:

I am perfect, holy, and good.

Just as I am. Just as I am.

Go, be at peace. I am healed.

Amen.

REFLECTION AND CURIOSITY

The following questions are meant to deepen and expand, invite and beckon thoughtful, compassionate, curious responses to the story and liturgy of Talliya and Ashera. Whether playing with these questions on your own or in a group setting, carve out space for journaling, collaging, or painting in response. If engaging in a group discussion, choose one or two questions, at most, to hold at the center of your sacred circle.

1. In what ways does your story connect with Talliya's and Ashera's story? What resonates? What draws you in?

2. When reading and praying along with Talliya and Ashera, what sensations do you notice in your body?

3. Healing comes in many forms. What does healing look like for you?

4. What does mental health mean to you? In what ways has your faith supported your mental health, and in what ways has your faith hindered it?

5. In what ways can you connect with and advocate for people healing from sexual assault?

PUBLIC WITNESS

Being able to access healing is everything. Without access, people continue to live isolated and in pain. The organizations highlighted below help create greater access to mental health care and advocacy to bring healing, hope, and safety to survivors.

The Loveland Foundation is committed to showing up for communities of color in unique and powerful ways with a particular focus on Black women and girls. Their resources and initiatives are collaborative, prioritizing opportunity, access, validation, and healing. In particular, with the barriers affecting access to treatment by members of diverse ethnic and racial groups, the Loveland Therapy Fund provides financial assistance to Black women and girls seeking therapy nationally.

Therapy for Black Girls seeks to sustain and grow an engaged community centered on the mental health needs of Black women and girls by creating resources, content, and experiences designed to present information in a way that feels relevant and accessible.

The **"me too" Movement** supports survivors of sexual violence and their allies by connecting survivors to resources, offering community organizing resources, pursuing a "me too" policy platform, and working with researchers to add to the field and chart a way forward. The "me too" Movement believes that help begins by connecting survivors to resources for healing, justice, action, and leadership.

Love Rises is a justice enterprise sponsored by **The Center for Contemplative Justice** that helps women refugees in war torn lands knit socks and blankets to reflect hope and become financially stable. Each knitted item holds a story of connection, of a single thread of yarn that is carefully hand-woven into a new product, and of connection between women refugees and the world.

Learn more about these organizations, and discover more about organizations and faith communities in your area doing the work of creating access to mental health care and supporting survivors of sexual violence and war. Connect. Learn. Give. Grow.[48]

---

[48] https://thelovelandfoundation.org/ and https://therapyforblackgirls.com/ and https://metoomvmt.org/ and https://www.tcfcj.org/currentprojects

TEN

Women's Easter

Mary Magdalene
Luke 24:1–11

HERSTORY

Very early in the morning on the first day of the week, the women went to the tomb, bringing the fragrant spices they had prepared. They found the stone rolled away from the tomb, but when they went in, they didn't find the body of the Lord Jesus. They didn't know what to make of this. Suddenly, two men were standing beside them in gleaming bright clothing. The women were frightened and bowed their faces toward the ground, but the men said to them, "Why do you look for the living among the dead? He isn't here, but has been raised. Remember what he told you while he was still in Galilee, that the Human One must be handed over to sinners, be crucified, and on the third day rise again." Then they remembered his words. When they returned from the tomb, they reported all these things to the eleven and all the others. It was Mary Magdalene, Joanna, Mary the mother of James, and the other women with them who told these things to the apostles. Their words struck the apostles as nonsense, and they didn't believe the women.[49]

* * *

In every birth there is death;

In every death there is birth.

---

[49] Luke 24:1–11, *Common English Bible.*

This is not a tit-for-tat system.
The universe does not need
our shallow attempts at balance.

Rather, it's a confession,
a sacrament of what is—
a universe that honors both
life and death, that testifies to the
sacredness of both coming and going,
that follows bedraggled, grieving women
to a death-sealed tomb only to find them,
moments later, running to tell whomever will
hear: "He is not here! He is risen!"

Life, then death, then life again.

Perhaps Easter is God's invitation
for us to embrace, not duality,
    but the complexity of such a reality.

Perhaps Easter is God's way of saying, yet again,
    "I am with you even
    unto the ends of the earth."[50]

---

[50] Matthew 28:20, *New International Version*.

Perhaps Easter is not to be explained but lived

in the pounding of feet upon a dusty path

toward a sun rising in the east,

giving birth to a new day,

    laying rest to the one that came before.

Perhaps Easter is about the women,

not so much because of what we do *for* you,

but because of who we are and what we carry—

the Good News that we need not conquer death

    in order to live.

We can, instead, be messengers

of love in both death and life, carrying oils that

consecrate and heal in every circumstance,

with everybody,

    everywhere.

* * *

I was born into a wealthy family and therefore married into a wealthy family. Wealth is friends with wealth. Rich people know other rich people. It is part of the sick cycle of poverty. The rich get richer; the poor get poorer, mostly because poor people have no access to where the money lives. The barriers, built intentionally, are too great to overcome.

I was painfully unaware of this sick cycle of poverty until I met Jesus. But once you know something that profound, that blatant, you can't unknow it. So when my husband died, I inherited his wealth (we had no children of our own, and he had no brothers), and I lived quite comfortably along the shore of Magdala. Any mention of me being demon-possessed is a limited perspective. I was a woman living freely, which, for a society hell-bent on keeping women anything but, proved troublesome.

"She is a witch," they would whisper.

"She is too much."

"She is not enough."

"Whore. Demon-possessed. Crazy. Unhinged."

All this because I was a wealthy widow who didn't remarry or have children. The lengths to which people will go to discount an independent woman would be comical if they weren't so painful.

I spent my time reading and dancing, kneading bread dough, and painting with oils. I joined other artists and there met Susanna and Joanna, other women of time and means who were also longing for community and companionship.

* * *

When I first met Jesus, I was walking along the shore, praying. A crowd had gathered in the distance, so I approached it cautiously, curious about what I'd find. The stench wafting from the congregation was what I encountered first. This was a smelly brood. Then, as I looked around, I noticed that this was not a normal gathering but a mishmash of fishermen, tax collectors, women, children, people of questionable character and rumored sin. Apparently, Jesus didn't care what company he kept.

He was preaching about a change of heart, about vulnerability, about the reign of God here and now for the least, the last, the lost. I couldn't look away or walk away, seized by the openness, the inclusion, the love.

Afterward, I approached Jesus, something women weren't supposed to do, and said, "I'd like to help you."

Our eyes met. We both smiled. It was the beginning of a beautiful friendship.

"How so?" Jesus asked.

"I have money, time, and faithfulness. I'd like to join you, if you're willing."

It was that simple and that profound. From that day forward, I was a disciple of and investor in Jesus. I also became his closest confidante, information the stories leave out lest the pure, holy Jesus be scandalized by the presence and position of a woman.

The fact that we women bleed and yet do not die has confounded men since the beginning of time. Though I have never experienced being pregnant, I know what it is to bleed every month, and I know what it is to live.

Because of the fear and hatred of women and our bodies, there was no friendship between men and women unless they were married or related. The collective imagination suffered greatly for its inability to conceive of trust, joy, and intimacy between a man and a woman that didn't include sex. Perhaps it still does.

Yet Jesus sought my counsel and heeded my wisdom as a friend. I was the one to whom he turned when he had a question about God, not because I gave him an answer but because I would listen. He learned early on to follow his mother and his sisters, that their dance with mystery held a power he wanted to know. It is fair to say, then, that his friendship with me was birthed because of them. Women: we're always leading one another to one another.

* * *

For close to three years, I gave my time, presence, and money to Jesus and his ministry. I traveled, baked bread, led artistic moments of freedom and rest among the disciples, and cared for the logistics of our growing movement. The bread he broke the night before he died is bread I made—a simple unleavened loaf, cooked over the fire, made with love.

The days were long, as were the nights. As Jesus gained notoriety, so did we. Who was this community of transient people following this man across the country? It was whole body, mind, and spirit work; work not for the faint of heart; work that begged questions from authorities and confusion from our loved ones and weariness within ourselves.

The days were also ripe with friendships and care like I'd never known. The last meal we shared together was one of the richest— bread broken, wine shared, bodies cleansed, lives consecrated and made whole.

Death lingered in the air that final night. I'd long ago learned not to fear it. We women know pain intimately; we learn at an early age that the best approach to it is not in war but in peace. Not in fight but in flow. Not in resistance but in surrender. In this way, Jesus was so much more woman than man in the traditional sense of these constructs.

"It will be what it will be. Into Your Spirit I commend my own."

It was my job to hold vigil, to witness, to love. It was my job to stand watch and eventually to testify. It was my job to bear whatever good news could be borne.

* * *

To say we were exhausted would be a shallow attempt at explaining the months of weariness we carried in our bodies, the days and hours of grief that set up camp within us, refusing to leave. To say we were traumatized would mean we were conscious of what we'd witnessed, that we'd had time to process it, that we were aware of what it meant and how it would affect us for years on end. To say all these things would be our facile attempt to ascribe meaning to an experience retrospectively—which is how we process trauma and heal.

But in the early morning hours after Jesus had been brutally murdered by the empire, all we knew were the rituals of death: that you do not leave a body alone; that you bless it with oil, wrap it in cloth, and accompany it to the tomb. All we knew was what we'd witnessed repeatedly from childhood when one of our loved ones died: how to keep vigil, take care, be present.

We needed no words. There was no waking; we'd been awake all night. Just as we'd seen our grandmothers do countless times before, we packed the oils, gathered the spices, wrapped our heads, and set out for the tomb.

With the morning still dark, we made our way to the tomb by instinct. Walking together, hand in hand, the only comfort we felt was the others' presence and the dim, dark light clawing its way through the clouds on the eastern horizon.

Because it was dark, we couldn't see that the stone seal had been rolled to the side and opened until we were upon it, standing in the threshold of outside and inside, earth and other.

We were accustomed to the dark. The dark was a place where we created our most beautiful treasures, where we had our most heartfelt conversations, where we loved and feasted, found silence and sanctuary. The dark was where we gave birth and died all at once, a sacrament of sacred reality. We women were accustomed to the dark.

I could smell the stench of death as we approached the tomb. Death and birth smell the same. Anyone who's been present when someone dies or when someone is born can testify to this reality. The smell is chemical, metallic, of the earth. This is why we bring spices and oils when a mother is in labor and when someone dies. The elements help cleanse and preserve, calm and heal. And they mask the smell.

The smell was both unsettling and comforting all at once. It was a reminder that only a thin veil separates life and death, and that a hope for something beyond always exists, even if we cannot see it.

Were we entering a tomb or a womb? Were we stumbling upon an ending or a beginning? Were we dying or living? Were we silent or singing?

Though Joanna raised her lamp for us to see inside, I'd already fallen to the ground, my hands acting as my eyes, searching for his body. On hands and knees, clawing at the dirt, I was desperate to find him. "Where is he?" I cried. "He's not here!"

The others joined me, raising their lanterns, searching for his frame.

Touching nothing but dirt, the earth to which he was returned, we sat stunned, silent.

Just as did Elijah in the cave at Horeb, we heard God not in the wailing or the clawing or the sifting but in the sound of a low whisper: "Why do you look for the living among the dead? He is not here. He has risen."[51]

We helped one another get to our feet, took a few moments to find our balance, and returned the way we'd come.

When we found the eleven disciples, the men, they were hiding in a thicket of trees outside of town. When we told them what we had seen and heard, they didn't believe us. We were used to not being believed. They had to see for themselves.

Perhaps all of us, in one way or another, must see for ourselves that which is unseeable. Perhaps all of us must discover what helps us hold on. Perhaps all of us need some time and space to claw through the dirt, grasping at something beyond our reach. Perhaps all of us need some time at the altar of what we do not know.

* * *

"Why didn't Jesus give you the keys to the kingdom, Auntie Mary?"

The children, gathered in a circle, never beat around the bush. They always cut to the core; they always know the heart of a matter.

"I don't know," I reply honestly.

I am old now and close to death. My time with the children is sacred. I still plant seeds, and I trust they will grow.

"I can imagine throwing the keys away," I say, "walking right up to the edge of a cliff and dropping them into the abyss. I imagine telling Jesus we don't need a head or key keeper at all, only a circle, ever widening, making all things new. I imagine a circle like the doorway of an empty tomb, to the roundness of a pregnant belly, to a birth canal, to a basket carrying spices and oils for consecrating and blessing both the living and the dead."

Their eyes grow large. Their heads nod. The inquisition continues.

"What was that first Easter morning like, Auntie Mary? Did you know Jesus had risen? Did you know his rising would change the world?"

---

[51] Luke 24:5–6, *New International Version*.

I am quiet for a long time.

I sit still.

I tell them I need a moment to think,

to feel.

It's tempting to impose certainty of meaning after the fact, to pretend we understand what was happening all along. But we must remember that all we knew in those wee hours of the morning, or as our friend and leader was being tortured and killed, was that the love, inclusion, openness, transformation, and vulnerability Jesus preached and lived threatened the Roman Empire. Indeed, these attributes threaten *every* empire.

To lay down our weapons means we drop our defenses, abandon all the fortresses we've built to make us feel worthy and powerful in order to protect us from vulnerability and weakness. To take the yoke of Jesus upon us means we rest in the softness of our skin and the ease of having nothing to prove. To repent means we quite literally change form. What we think of as "ours" becomes "theirs," and what we think of as "mine" becomes "everyone's." Empires fall when we follow Jesus. Dictators are eliminated. The reign of God really does come on earth as it is in heaven.

So when I think back to that first Easter morning, I don't think of it as Easter at all. Instead, I think of it as the first day without him physically present by our sides. I think of it as a fog of grief, a thunderstorm of disorientation, an ocean of question marks.

I did not intend to be the apostle to the apostles. It's odd how devotion can put you in a role you never thought you'd inhabit. In those early days, I couldn't begin to imagine what a community of faith in Jesus might look like, though I imagined it would feel like coming home. Our purpose—the need to heal from our grief—gave us something to do together. The vision would come later.

What felt most healing during the long nights when our memories tormented us was the confession that Jesus didn't have to die so that we might live. It felt wrong that our salvation required is death. No. In whatever ways Jesus lived in us and through us was a testament to his life, not to his brutal death. And so we began to imagine a world in which no one needed to die so that we could live. We dreamt about this world, claimed it, dared to preach about it just as Jesus did. And out of that communal grief and imagination, a community began to form.

Led by the women carrying oils and spices to anoint the living and the dead, what marked this community was its purpose to help us heal. Sitting with others in pain, holding space for questions, listening deeply to what people needed, the first church was women's church and required no steeple at all, only a gathering of heart-weary disciples intent on keeping vigil, taking care, and being present just as we were on the dark morning after Jesus was killed, just as every woman had done for centuries for their beloved.

With all these thoughts and experiences floating through my mind, body, and spirit, I pull the children close to me around the fire, our blankets draped across our shoulders and laps, the coolness of spring still lingering in the air. I am their old auntie, their wise woman, their wisdom teacher, their elder, their storyteller.

Drawing them near, I say, "If it weren't for the women, we wouldn't have any of this. Easter is a celebration of mystery, a confession of all we do not know, an invitation to love. This is not the end," I say. "We're still writing the story together."

There's a little girl sitting to my left, nodding her head. She reaches for a scrap of papyrus and a pen, gifts I'd given her. She begins to write—what, I do not know. But I imagine it has something to do with life, something to do with death, and something to do with us showing up in love for both.

LITURGY FOR MORNING PRAYER

OPENING

If and when possible, practice this liturgy at sunrise. If you are gathered with others, gather yourselves in a circle. Place a candle in the center. If you are alone, light a candle as a sign of connection to the circle of women saints who join you, even now, as you pray.

Morning Greeting

> Today is the day we are given.
>
> We've not known this day before,
>
> We will not know it again;
>
> Let us rejoice and be glad.

Morning Prayer

> Before the sun rises in the east, You are there.
>
> Before the women walk to the river, You are there.
>
> Before the living bury the dead, You are there.
>
> **After the party ends, You are there.**
>
> **After the drive home, You are there.**
>
> **After the long, dark night, You are there.**
>
> We rise to greet You,
>
> giving thanks for your presence in every place of our lives.
>
> **No matter how we wake or where we go this day,**
>
> **You are with us,**
>
> **May Your name be praised,**
>
> **And Your love be shared**
>
> **with everyone, everywhere.**
>
> **Amen.**

Psalm 118:1–4, 26–29 (inspired by the *Common English Bible* translation)

> **With thanksgiving, we come to You,**
> **O God, our Mother.**
> **Your love is with us forever.**
> Let the children of Leah and Rachel say,
>> "Her love is with us forever!"
>
> **Let the house of Elisheba say,**
>> **"Her love is with us forever!"**
>
> Let those who revere you say,
>> "Her love is with us forever!"
>
> **Blessed is she who walks to the tomb,**
> **Who enters your womb,**
> **Who longs to be reborn.**
> Bow down before the light,
> Honor the holy dark.
> Make altars as you go.
> For everywhere is sacred.
> **You are our Mother, our God,**
> **And we thank You for giving us life.**
> **You are worthy of our praise.**
> With thanksgiving, we come to You,
> O God, our Mother.
> Your love is with us forever.

Scripture Reading: Luke 24:1–11

> The Word of life.
> **Thanks be to God.**
> *Silence*

Prayers of the People

> In peace, let us pray.
> **Have mercy**

For the joy of the world . . .

Have mercy

For the peace of the world . . .

Have mercy

For the women of the world . . .

Have mercy

For the children of the world . . .

Have mercy

For the hungry of the world . . .

Have mercy

For the traumatized ones of the world . . .

Have mercy on us.

For the leaders of the world . . .

Have mercy

For the farmers of the world . . .

Have mercy

For the enemies that we know, for the enemies that we do not know . . .

Have mercy

For ourselves . . .

Have mercy

For the saints and sinners who've gone before us . . .

Have mercy

By Your love deliver us into the world anew.

Moment of Silence

In the communion of God, our Mother,

Spirit, our Sister, and

Christ, our Daughter,

We entrust ourselves into wholehearted living and dying.

Amen.

Song of Praise

"Blessed Is She"
Words and music by Claire K. McKeever-Burgett

The following song can be sung several times through in the practice of meditative singing, the repetition of which offers a deeper connection to God and to the women who are to be followed and whose stories are to be believed.

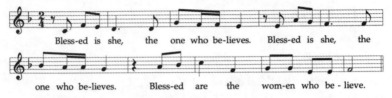

Bless-ed is she, the one who be-lieves. Bless-ed is she, the one who be-lieves. Bless-ed are the wom-en who be-lieve.

Contemporary Connection

Take a few moments to watch and listen to "A Little Revival," by Radney Foster.[52] *Imagine Mary and the children singing and dancing to this song on the hillside on Easter morning. Dance and sing with them!*

The Prayer of Mary (inspired by Luke 1:46–55)

O Mother God, we glorify You.

From the depths of our beings, we rejoice in You,

Our Deliverer.

As You show mercy to us, help us show mercy to others.

As You honor our bodies, help us honor all other bodies.

As You scatter the deceitful and remove tyrants from their thrones,

help us work for justice and shalom.

Fill the hungry with good things.

Show us what is enough.

Deliver us from pride into mercy.

Deliver us from evil into love.

---

[52] https://www.youtube.com/watch?v=zLjLy51AsMc

For Yours is the birthing room, the power, the vulnerability,

the glory, and the love,

eternally here, eternally now.

Amen.

Closing Blessing

May joy awaken your heart.

May peace remind you of your mother's womb.

May justice spark a flame.

May love help it catch fire.

May the God of joy, peace, justice, and love

Hold you and love you forever. **Amen.**

REFLECTION AND CURIOSITY

The following questions are meant to deepen and expand, invite and beckon thoughtful, compassionate, curious responses to the story and liturgy of Mary Magdalene. Whether playing with these questions on your own or in a group setting, carve out space for journaling, collaging, or painting in response. If engaging in a group discussion, choose one or two questions, at most, to hold at the center of your sacred circle.

1. In what ways does your story connect with Mary Magdalene's story? What resonates with you? What draws you in?

2. When reading and praying along with Mary Magdalene, what sensations do you notice in your body?

3. What legacy do you hope to create alongside your loved ones, and what legacy have you already created? Name it. Own it. Claim it in all its particularity.

4. How do you understand leadership? What kind of leader are you? What kind of leader do you long to be?

5. What does women's Easter mean to you?

PUBLIC WITNESS

Where are women gathering to share the good news, act in good faith, and promote social justice?

United Women of Faith works to improve the lives of women, children, and youth around the world. They connect spiritual women to act boldly for justice and to transform communities. Their work to "Celebrate International Day of the Girl Child" advocates for healthy food and clean water, access to sexual and reproductive health care, equitable education and quality curricula in a safe environment, and freedom from child marriage, body mutilation, and exploitation.

Young Clergy Women International (YWCI) creates a holy and authentic community that sustains generous collaboration for Christian clergy women under the age of forty. In particular, YCWI values kinship, embodiment, nurture, and the championing of women as they witness a resurrection first preached by women.

Learn more about these particular organizations, and discover more about organizations and faith communities in your own area doing the work of leading, witnessing, and advocating for women and girls in creative, collaborative, and justice-centered ways. Connect. Learn. Give. Grow.[53]

---

[53] https://uwfaith.org/ and https://youngclergywomen.org/about/our-mission-and-values/

Part Three

Content Warning: Traumatic Birth, Fertility/Infertility

The memories come to me in flashes: How I threw off my clothes like they were trash; how I climbed, like an animal, on top of the bed; how my doctor, typically calm, cool, and collected, jumped on top of me and pressed her hands into my belly in an attempt to move you, my baby, down and out; how I screamed, "Is she alive? Am I alive?" gasping for air; how your heart rate started to drop; how I bled over a liter of blood; how every person in the room chorused, "Push!"; how some of the ones screaming were beyond the veil, visiting me from the other, mysterious side; how nurses stuck me over and over and over again, unable to get a needle in a vein; how my doctor looked me in the eyes and said, "I'm gonna have to knock you out"; how I spread my arms wide and said, "Take me."

How, in the end, it was the forceps specialist who found your head and ripped you out of me. You were sunny-side up, staring at the ceiling, wide-eyed and ready.

If it sounds violent, it's because it was. I arrived at the hospital fully dilated to ten centimeters, and though I cried for drugs, there was very little time and no needle that could find a vein for my body to be spared the intense pain of delivering you into this world.[54]

---

[54] There are approximately 6,300 births at St. Thomas Midtown Hospital in Nashville, Tennessee, every year, and according to my physician, Dr. Amanda Barrett, they almost never use forceps or even a vacuum, which is a less bulky instrument than forceps, without anesthetizing the person giving birth. It is fair to say that I was an emergent exception. To bring Liv into the world, they used forceps, and I was not medicated.

Sometimes life will, quite literally, rip you in two. Life can also be the thing that puts you back together. I will spend the rest of my days marveling at this mystery—how what breaks you can mend you; how what almost kills you can restore you to life.[55] As painful and terrifying and traumatic as so much of bringing you into this world was, I'd do it all over again in a heartbeat, which doesn't make me a masochist or a martyr but a mother. And I am grateful to be yours.

* * *

Our journey to Liv Katherine McKeever-Burgett, our daughter who was born on September 5, 2019, was a long one. All told, it took approximately 760 days for her to get here, or two years and one month. After experiencing what doctors call "secondary infertility" with no explanation of why—my blood work was normal; my husband's sperm counts were normal—after taking my temperature every morning for months to track my ovulation cycle, after attending God knows how many acupuncture visits, after lighting every candle I could find, after praying thousands of times and crying oceans of tears, after letting go one day only to pick it back up the next, I got a positive result on a pregnancy test in December 2018. It felt both miraculous and ordinary, both unreal and exactly as it should be.

I loved being pregnant. I loved growing large. I loved taking up space. In a world in which large is considered wrong, taking up space is discouraged, and pregnancy is seen as a transitory phase instead of its own sacred existence, I reveled in the reality of growing a life within my body. It felt like my superpower. I felt similarly when pregnant with our first child, Wade, though something about knowing this would be my last pregnancy, as well as something about the long journey to get there, made me extra aware of every sensation, every movement, and every breath.

---

[55] Please note the word *can* in this sentence. In no way do I seek to offer platitudes in the vein of "what doesn't kill you makes you stronger." Rather, I mean to speak of my experience giving birth to Liv and the subsequent healing from it. In no way do I think life always mends us or that suffering, trauma, and pain are essential for a redemptive life. Suffering is not redemptive; it is suffering. How we heal together in the aftermath can be redemptive, and for my own redemptive moments amid deep pain, I am grateful.

Liv's guess date (the date health care providers guess a baby will come based on a birthing person's ovulation cycle) was two days after Wade's on August 25. Wade arrived on his guess date, August 23, 2015, so the chance that I'd give birth on Wade's birthday felt like a strong possibility. However, August 23 came and went. As did August 25 and eleven full days after it before Liv made her entrance on the earth.

Take everything you've ever heard about second babies coming sooner, then throw it out the window. In fact, take everything you've ever heard about most anything related to giving birth and let it go too. If I know anything, it's that neither we nor anyone else has any control over how or when or why babies arrive in this world. Doctors will pretend that they do, but they don't. In the end, they're just as confused as we are. In the end, I was wise to spread my arms, take a deep breath, and say, "Take me."

* * *

Wade Aaron McKeever-Burgett joined us in an emergent way too. Though I labored with him for close to twenty-three hours, I ended up needing an emergency C-section because his heart rate was continuing to plummet.

"We've never known a birth that isn't an emergency," Adam said in the days after Liv was born.

I'd be lying if I said I had an immediate peace about this truth. I'd be lying if I acted as if it didn't sting—as if I had control over how my babies came into this world, as if it was my fault that for one birth I had to be cut open and for another birth I had to be ripped open. Yet this is exactly how I felt. Sometimes, in the shadowy, vulnerable moments, I still feel this way.

At my six-week checkup after Wade was born, the midwife said to me, "It's not your fault you had a C-section." Her comment surprised me because I didn't think I was asking for this reassurance. But something in the way I'd showed up must have prompted her to say it. But if it wasn't my fault, whose fault was it? I couldn't help but think that someone or something needed to be blamed for how my child was brought into this world, and wasn't I the likely target given that he came from my body, my flesh?

I walk around acting like the world is on my shoulders, like it's all up to me, like I'm the only one in charge of everything. I don't mean to act this way, yet it is so deeply baked into our culturalization and construction as women.[56] I'm often already down the road before I realize where I am: floating on an island, alone, taking on the world and its problems by myself, unconsciously trying to ensure it's not my fault, that I'm not the one to blame. Though self-reliance is surely not what God intended, it's the way my central nervous system is conditioned to operate.

Early on in our journey to become pregnant a second time, I began regular spiritual direction with Marjorie Thompson, whom I knew through my work at The Upper Room and with The Academy for Spiritual Formation. We met monthly, and I would drive to her house, blaring Beyoncé from the speakers of my car before turning it off, taking a deep breath, and walking up the sidewalk to her front door.

I'd knock softly, the rhythm of Beyoncé still beating in my chest.

Marjorie would open the door with a smile on her face and say, "Welcome."

Sometimes I would hear a soft violin or the low hum of a cello playing in the background, though neither of those instruments was present, and Marjorie certainly didn't play music during our sessions. Where Beyoncé meets the symphony is where I met spiritual direction with Marjorie—a beautiful, seemingly disparate pairing that makes a whole lot of sense when it takes place.

In spiritual direction, she asked me questions that didn't require answers, but only my attention, my noticing, my breath, my prayer. In spiritual direction, I learned how to sit still, slow down, and listen. In spiritual direction, I was deconditioned to the idea of individual responsibility and instead invited into a communal spirituality that helped me trust that I've never been and never will be alone.

"What does it feel like to trust what you do not know?"

"How might you lean on the understanding of your better angels who pray and dance and live and breathe on your behalf?"

---

[56] https://www.theguardian.com/world/2015/nov/08/women-gender-roles-sexism-emotional-labor-feminism

"What does self-compassion look like for you? How can you be kinder and gentler with yourself today, and how might that help you be kinder and gentler with others?"

Marjorie's questions began to teach me that it's not all up to me. I could sit in the presence of my discomfort and fear without having all the answers (or any answers at all) and not die. Rather, the discomfort and the fear might help me live.

For this reason, I've built altars throughout our home. In each room there's a candle, a photo, an icon, a stone from a riverside, a piece of artwork one of our children created. Wherever I go in our home, these small, holy places remind me that I am connected to St. Clare, Our Lady of Guadalupe, my grandparents, my children, my parents, my brother, my nieces, my friends, the women, the land, and God. My body, kneeling at the altar, touching stones and photos and icons with my actual hands, reminds me of others' bodies and how I might show up alongside them in the struggle for freedom.

Daily prayer, then, is a connection, not an isolation. Daily mindfulness is an act of community, not an act of individualization. Embodied spiritual practice—walking around my home, kneeling at these little altars everywhere—serves as an antidote to a white supremacist patriarchal system designed to keep us isolated, alone, and thinking we're individually responsible for everything.

This ancient Proverb keeps ringing in my ears: "Trust in the LORD with all your heart and lean not on your own understanding; in all your ways submit to the LORD, and the LORD will make your paths straight."[57] Through a prayerful reading of this scripture, I now hear a different translation:

> *Trust in Love and know that your understanding of the world is not the only one. When you follow Love, there is always more to learn about yourself and about others. When you lean on Love, you see, not a straight path but a whole one, accompanied by other pilgrims who trust in Love alongside you.*

* * *

[57] Proverbs 3:5–6, *New International Version*.

I'm sitting in my counselor's office with my eyes closed, one hand on my heart, one on my belly. She's invited me to conjure a peaceful scene in my mind's eye, a place to which I can return when I need to self-regulate and find calm.

The sun is low in the sky, setting on the West Texas horizon. I stand in an open field, surrounded by pale-yellow, dry grass, wily mesquite trees, and dust. There is a small creek bed where shallow water flows, and when I look to my left, I see a brown cow resting under a tree. She has pecan-shaped black eyes that wrap me like a blanket. She says, "Being who you are is your birthright." I say, "Thank you."

When the memories come like flashes, and I can't sleep, I place one hand on my heart and one on my belly. I conjure the cow. I hear her wisdom. I breathe.[58]

* * *

When Wade was three years old, all I wanted was to be pregnant with another child, to offer a sibling for my son and grow our family. One night, a pile of rocks fell out of his pockets as I helped him undress before bath time.

"What are these?" I asked.

"Rocks for my sister," Wade replied.

"What?" I said, trying to catch my breath.

"Rocks for my sister," Wade said again. "I'm collecting them for her."

I stammered an okay, said we'd work on that together, and then continued with his bath and bedtime.

Later that night as I lit my candles, Our Lady of Guadalupe shimmering from her place on our family altar, I asked her, "Is this a joke?"

She whispered, "Of course not."

---

[58] This vision took place while practicing Eye Movement Desensitization and Reprocessing (EMDR) with a trained professional. Learn more about EMDR here: https://www.emdr.com/what-is-emdr/.

I knew enough of surrender to get on my knees, let the tears flow, and ask for help in trusting the wisdom and knowing of my child. Who was I to say what Wade did and didn't know?

When I finally was pregnant with Liv and we shared the news with Wade, he reached out his hand, touched my heart, and said, "Is this where she is?"

I nodded yes and gently moved his hand down to the soft skin just below my belly button. "She's in here too," I said.

To this day, when both of my children press their bodies into mine, finding the soft curve of my belly, the roll of my side, the warmth of my chest, I remember what Jesus commanded and what the prophets foretold: *Let the children come to me* and *A child will lead them.* I have no doubt that the prophet's wisdom came from, for, and by the women. When my children touch my heart and my belly, the places from which they were born, I remember, *The children know,* and *I am wise to follow their knowing.*

* * *

In the days after Liv's birth, I feel shell-shocked, which is to be "mentally confused, upset, or exhausted as a result of a highly stressful or disturbing and often unexpected event or experience," as Merriam-Webster describes it.[59]

The pain I feel in my body is unbearable. Constant throbbing, very little relief. It's difficult to stand up straight; it's impossible to lie down comfortably. The postpartum care I receive from the nursing staff in the hospital just after Liv is born is subpar. My pain is questioned, my experience discounted, evidence of an overburdened, broken medical system and the patriarchal, misogynistic culture in which it was created and sustained. Thankfully, my doctor sits on the side of my bed, looks me in the eye, and treats me like a human being. Thankfully, she listens to me and ensures that the nurses are attentive and kind for the remainder of my hospital stay.

I keep thinking that if I were a Woman of Color in this much pain with this traumatic of a birth, it would likely be even worse. It's

---

[59] https://www.merriam-webster.com/dictionary/shell-shocked

amply documented that Women of Color are less likely to be believed about their pain and that Black women suffer disproportionately at the hands of our medical system.[60] This reality doesn't discount my pain or my experience, but it does intensify it and, even more than I did prior to bringing Liv into the world, makes me want to burn to the ground white, male, heterosexist, patriarchal systems.

My mother moves in with us to help me heal. My father returns to Texas to tend to things back home. I weep the day he leaves; his tenderness and empathy are almost too much to bear. I see in his eyes and feel in his embrace his knowledge of physical pain and trauma due to his own open-heart surgeries (one when he was twenty-three, the other when he was forty) to replace a malfunctioning aortic valve with which he was born. My parents are living proof that we heal together. They are living proof that gentleness and love, compassion and care can live in all of us. Without my parents, I am not me; without me, my parents are not them.

* * *

Liv is tiny and snuggled to my breast. The miracle of feeding her from my body will never not astound me. How we women are not carried around on soft pillows and revered for the powerful creatures that we are is beyond me. What I know is that we seek to control that which we fear, and we fear that which we do not understand. This is what's been happening to women for centuries. We humans have been doing this to God since the beginning of time: trying to confine God to a box, a temple, a gender, a church building, or a pew; trying to take the uncontainable and contain it; trying to take the mystery and solve it.

Though I do not mistake women for the Divine, we women do contain divinity. And while I do not conflate the holy of holies with the ones who've kept the Earth spinning since the beginning, I do celebrate, honor, recognize, and name women's lives for what they are: sacred.

* * *

---

[60] https://www.washingtonpost.com/health/is-bias-keeping-female-minority-patients-from-getting-proper-care-for-their-pain/2019/07/26/9d1b3a78-a810-11e9-9214-246e594de5d5_story.html

It is safe to say that writing this book has been a significant part of my healing. Listening deeply to women's voices and stories, asking them what it is they want and need to say, offering a sacred, safe place for them to say it, is good. And where there is goodness, there is God. Where there is God, there is Love. Where there is Love, there is healing.

May healing be ours, together. Amen.

As we come to a close, may we continue to be open to learning new truths from old stories. May those new truths take hold of us and inform how we move through the world.

As we finish reading and speaking the words, may they stir our hearts like communion wine

tingling at the back of our throats. May those words evoke new thoughts and ideas that call us

to live deeply.

As we consume the liturgies, may they form us to live courageously and curiously, knowing that there is still much to learn, and to unlearn, in our lives of faith.

Gracious and loving God, the Source of all love and spirit, we offer thanks and praise for Claire, and the spirit that calls her to feel so deeply the stories of women in Scripture and to share

them so generously. Thank you for the life and witness of all the women, known and unknown,

past and present, who carry the story of faith into the world and bear the truth that love is the

most powerful source for change. Thank you for the gift of this book and for every life touched

by its creation, its reading, and its practice.

May we readers find new hope, strength, and truth, and carry it with us all the days of our lives. And may the blessing of the One who creates, sustains, and comforts reside in us always.

Amen.

—Becca Stevens, founder of Thistle Farms

Appendix

GLOSSARY

Liturgy—Liturgy means "the work of the people of God." When we, the people, practice a liturgy, we practice the work of God, hoping that our practice together in sacred space will be what and how we practice together in the whole of our lives. For example, when we pray the prayers and stories of women in a worship service, the goal is that those prayers and stories translate to being with and for women outside of the worship service—at the polls and our dinner tables, in our parent-teacher conferences, and in conversations with our children. The praying, singing, scripture reading, candle lighting, and story-sharing is ours to practice, share, and engage, both inside and outside of the church walls. In this way, then, practicing, speaking, praying, saying, and singing the liturgy together is an essential part of the transformation of ourselves and of the whole wide world. What good are our prayers on Sunday if they hold no meaning in our lives on Monday?

Midrash—Midrash is a rabbinic mode of interpretation, commentary, or exegesis found in many early rabbinic collections, the largest being the work of *Midrash Rabbah*. First practiced among rabbis between 400 and 1200 CE, Midrash helped fill in the gaps of the biblical narrative. Midrash is the story beyond the story, the digging deeper, the exploration of meaning. The practice of midrash enables those left out to claim their place within the narrative, to find their voice and use it, to illuminate a whole host of truth, and experience beyond what men canonized centuries ago—largely for their fellow men.

Prayer—Prayer is a connection with God, love, holiness, other. This means that prayer can be everywhere and always. Perhaps the instruction in 1 Thessalonians 5:16 to "Pray without ceasing" is less an admonition to pray for twenty-four hours a day and more an invitation to recognize our very lives as living prayers.

When we rinse the dishes, we pray. When we drive the kids to school, we pray. When we share a meal, we pray. When we send an email, we pray. Prayer is an unceasing opportunity to connect with the God who is ever-present, right here and right now. In this way, prayer is not a division of labor; it is the very labor itself. It works on behalf of the life, vision, and voice we wish to share with the world.

Sacred Space—Anywhere you feel a connection to the divine is sacred. A walk in the woods, a birthing room, a sick person's bedside, a wooden booth in a coffee shop. Spirit, after all, is everywhere. Sometimes, creating a sacred space or altar with a candle, photo of a loved one, or special stone can help facilitate connection to the divine and maintain our daily spiritual practice.

Scripture—More than the Bible we hold in our hands, which was canonized by men with texts written largely for and by them, *Scripture*, deeply influenced by the practice of midrash, is something we can tend with our words, prayers, insights, and longings. It is something to which we can bring our whole selves in an eagerness to learn and illuminate that which lies beyond. Less fixture and more flame, Scripture is that which reveals stories of liberation and love.

Spiritual Practice—Often likened to a path or journey that seeks to draw an individual or group of people closer to the divine, *spiritual practice* includes prayer, liturgy, meditation, movement, scripture reading and discovery, play, and community. These are simply a few of the elements of spiritual practice. Spiritual practice contains multitudes, and while it can be beautifully communal, it can also be deeply personal. The practices that allow you to connect with Spirit, love, and God may not be the practices that enable connection for others. That's the real gift of it: spiritual practice can be as unique as you are.

SMALL GROUP GUIDE

The small group guide offers a structure and rhythm for engaging each chapter of this book with a small group of people. I recommend gathering in circles of no more than six to ensure group cohesion and connection. Women have been gathering in circles for centuries, so it feels right to follow their lead and do the same.

Pre-Gathering

1. Of the six or fewer participants, one person will serve as Convener for each week. Invite each person to sign up for the week that works best for them to serve in this role. Encourage each member of the group to serve as Convener at least once. Because there are ten women's stories, four people will serve as Convener twice.

2. The Weekly Convener is responsible for ensuring the group knows which story it will be reading for the week, for bringing a candle for the center of the small group circle, and for ensuring that all members have a copy of the book and therefore of the Liturgy and Reflection Questions for that particular chapter/ story.

3. The Weekly Convener will also share the Group Guidelines with the group each week as a reminder of the values and principles that guide their engagement and discussion together.

Group Guidelines[61]

The Weekly Convener of the first gathering will begin by sharing the Group Guidelines. The Convener will hold space for group members to respond to the Group Guidelines, inviting clarifying questions and giving any additional guidance group members may need in order to feel seen and held in the group space. Weekly Conveners for following gatherings will likewise begin by reading aloud the Group Guidelines and asking if anyone has anything they need to add, signaling that these are living, breathing Guidelines subject to change if and as needed for the safety of the whole.

1. Speak using "I" statements and from your own personal, lived experience.

2. When confused about something, get curious. Use phrases like, "Tell me more," and "I'd love to hear more about _____."

[61] These Group Guidelines came into being because of my work and practice with The Academy for Spiritual Formation and The Center for Courage and Renewal. They also developed because I've been sitting with women in circles for years where we've trusted our intuition, wisdom, and love to guide, hold, and create safety to share our most honest, vulnerable, and brave stories.

3. Don't assume you know what someone else is thinking or feeling. It's always best to ask them rather than to assume you know on their behalf.

4. What is said in the group stays in the group. This also means that what is said in the group is not to be discussed with others in the group outside of the group setting and that from week to week, something said the week prior is only okay to reference if the person who said it says it again and invites reflection on it. In short, hold people's stories, comments, questions, and reflections with the utmost care, confidentiality, and discretion.

5. Release the need for certainty and instead embrace mystery. Practice saying, "I don't know" or "I'm still figuring out how I feel about that" when presented with a complex or difficult idea or question.

6. Allow room to breathe. Get comfortable with silence. Allow space after each person speaks.

7. If and when sharing a personal experience that contains sensitive and potentially activating content, offer a warning before sharing so that others in the group can make their own decision whether they can hear it or not.

8. Avoid cross talk and the impulse to try to "fix" someone else. We gather first to listen and then to respond. The main goal of being together is not to debate a particular topic or to fix one another; rather, it is to hold space for our stories, curiosities, and experiences to be spoken aloud. Even if you resonate deeply with what someone has shared or have a resource you are certain will help, resist the impulse to speak, and let the quiet speak for you.

9. Share by invitation, not demand. Listen to your own wisdom about when and what and how you need to speak (or not) into the circle.

10. Finally, be as present as possible. Silence your phone. Eliminate any other distractions. For the time the group gathers, commit to keeping your attention as undivided as your mind, body, and spirit allow.

Gathering

Below is the format to use when gathering in your small group for liturgy, prayer, and reflection. The format works best when held no fewer than sixty minutes and no longer than eighty minutes.

1. CIRCLE: Group members gather in a circle. The Weekly Convener lights the candle in the middle of the circle.

2. LITURGY: Each gathering begins by practicing the liturgy from the chapter you'll be discussing during your time together. Though the liturgies are titled *morning*, *midday*, *evening*, and *night*, they can be practiced at any time of the day, whenever your group meets. The Weekly Convener will read the regular typeface lines from the liturgy, and group members will read the bold typeface lines. Allow fifteen to twenty minutes to practice and pray the liturgy together.

3. BODY BREAK: After the liturgy concludes, invite a five-minute body break for stretching, going to the bathroom, deep breathing, etc.

4. WEEKLY CHECK-IN: As the group reconvenes, invite a twelve-minute check-in asking each member to respond to the question: "What's the past week been like for you?" (Each person has two minutes to share, so invite comments that are short and to the point.)

5. DEEPER REFLECTION: For the next thirty to forty minutes, engage the "Deeper Reflection" questions at the end of the chapter you're discussing for the week. The Weekly Convener will ask the first question and hold space for group members to respond. Here is when the Group Guidelines are particularly important to remember and follow. Group members will respond from their own experiences and will allow silence and space between each person's sharing. The Weekly Convener will determine when to move to the next question, and/or the group can decide together ahead of time which questions they want to discuss. There is no need to finish all of the questions; engaging only one or two questions may be enough for the meeting. The Weekly Convener will pay attention to the time, and when the deeper reflection time comes to a close, the group will say these words together:

We honor both what has been said and what has remained unsaid in this sacred circle, and we hold one another's stories, lives, hearts, and beings with respect, gratitude, and love. Until next time, may the God of joy and justice, liturgy and love hold us, comfort us, and guide us to people and places we never thought we'd go. Amen.

1. PUBLIC WITNESS: Invite group members to share one way they will practice the liturgy in their daily lives in the week ahead (voting, giving money to a woman-centered organization, etc.) This should take approximately five minutes.

2. CLOSING: The Weekly Convener will choose how to close the circle by choosing one of the prayers from the week's liturgy by saying *The Prayer of Mary*, or some other short blessing to end the time together. After a closing blessing, the Weekly Convener will blow out the center candle, indicating that the small group gathering has concluded.

BLESSED ARE THE WOMEN PLAYLIST

The following songs were on repeat during the writing of this book, and they're the songs that have been on repeat for most of my life, helping me breathe, reminding me to dance, inviting me to play, teaching me how to feel. The QR code will take you to the ***Blessed Are the Women* Playlist** on Spotify, where you, too, can put them on repeat, roll the windows down, or put your AirPods in, and dance, move, breathe, and be with the beat and the magic of the music.

*   "Like a Girl" by Lizzo
*   "Freedom" by Beyoncé
*   "You Make Me Feel Like a Natural Woman" by Carole King

- "Respect" by Aretha Franklin
- "Let Him Fly" by Patty Griffin
- "Wide Open Spaces" by The Chicks
- "Forgiveness" by Patty Griffin
- "Video" by India Arie
- "Standing" by Patty Griffin
- "Dark Runs Out" by Amy Stroup
- "Gaslighter" by The Chicks
- "Landslide" by Stevie Nicks
- "Everywhere" by Fleetwood Mac
- "When Will I Be Loved" by Linda Ronstadt
- "Closer to Fine" by Indigo Girls
- "CHURCH GIRL" by Beyoncé
- "I Would Die 4 U" by Rose Cousins, Bear's Den, Christof Van Der Ven
- "I Would Die 4 U" by Prince
- "One Voice" by The Wailin' Jennys
- "Wildflowers" by The Wailin' Jennys
- "Girl on Fire" by Alicia Keys
- "Better Life" by P!nk
- "I Am Here" by P!nk
- "Love Goes" by Sam Smith (feat. Labrinth)
- "Good Kisser" by Lake Street Drive
- "Daddy Lessons" by Beyoncé
- "All Night" by Beyoncé
- "Brave" by Sara Bareilles

- "Armor" by Sara Bareilles
- "Cover Me Up" by Jason Isbell
- "Burn" from *Hamilton* by Lin-Manuel Miranda
- "Who Lives, Who Dies, Who Tells Your Story?" from *Hamilton* by Lin-Manuel Miranda
- "Sexual Healing" by Hot 8 Brass Band
- "All Too Well" (10-Minute Version) (Swift's Version) by Taylor Swift
- "Woman" by Kesha
- "Good as Hell" by Lizzo
- "Sunday" by Joy Oladokun
- "Sacred" by Nina Nesbitt
- "This Feeling" by Alabama Shakes
- "Cowboy Take Me Away" by The Chicks
- "Humble and Kind" by Lori McKenna
- "Somebody to Love" by Queen
- "We Shall Not Be Moved" by Mavis Staples
- "Easy On Me" by Adele
- "Light On" by Maggie Rogers
- "Fallingwater" by Maggie Rogers

BLESSED ARE THE WOMEN READING LIST

Though it's only now appeared in print, I've been writing *Blessed Are the Women* my entire life. The following reading list both formed and still forms me (and therefore this book). It's a list of writings that I've been reading and rereading for years as a hope, prayer, and act of resistance. It is the list I will give my children when they start to ask questions of their lives and their faith. It's the list I give to myself repeatedly in the noise of the night and the quiet of the morning.

Rather than being comprehensive, it's personal and particular to me and my life.

Like this book, may this reading list be an invitation to deeper exploration and formation into your own story.

- *The Dance of the Dissident Daughter* by Sue Monk Kidd

- *The Body Is Not an Apology* by Sonya Renee Taylor

- *Midrash: Reading the Bible with Question Marks* by Sandy Eisenberg Sasso

- *The Red Tent* by Anita Diamant

- *Little Altars Everywhere* by Rebecca Wells

- *Moses, Man of the Mountain* by Zora Neale Hurston

- *Dancing with God* by Karen Baker-Fletcher

- *The Color Purple* by Alice Walker

- *Praying with the Psalms* by Nan C. Merrill

- *In the Sanctuary of Women: A Companion for Reflection and Prayer* by Jan L. Richardson

- *The Complete Psalms: The Book of Prayer Songs in a New Translation* by Pamela Greenberg

- *The Upper Room Worshipbook: Music and Liturgies for Spiritual Formation* compiled and edited by Elise S. Eslinger

- *Abuelita Faith: What Women on the Margins Teach Us About Wisdom, Persistence, and Strength* by Kat Armas

- *Dakota: A Spiritual Geography* by Kathleen Norris

- *Swallow's Nest: A Feminine Reading of the Psalms* by Marchiene Vroon Rienstra

- *The Beauty Myth: How Images of Beauty Are Used Against Women* by Naomi Wolf

- *Teaching to Transgress* by bell hooks

- *Poet Warrior: A Memoir* by Joy Harjo

- *The Long Loneliness: The Autobiography of the Legendary Catholic Social Activist* by Dorothy Day

- *What Kind of Woman* by Kate Baer

- *Cries of the Spirit: Poems in Celebration of Women's Spirituality* edited by Marilyn Sewell

- *Walking on Water: Reflections on Faith and Art* by Madeleine L'Engle

- *To Pray and to Love: Conversations on Prayer with the Early Church* by Roberta Bondi

- *Shrill* by Lindy West

- *Church in the Round: Feminist Interpretation of the Church* by Letty M. Russell

- *Also a Mother: Work and Family as Theological Dilemma* by Bonnie J. Miller-McLemore

- *The Body of God: An Ecological Theology* by Sallie McFague

- *Motherhood: A Confession* by Natalie Carnes

- *Sisters in the Wilderness: Challenges of Womanist God-Talk* by Delores S. Williams

- *Black Womanist Ethics* by Katie Geneva Cannon

- *Revelation* and *The River* by Flannery O'Connor

- *Womanist Theological Ethics* edited by Katie Geneva Cannon, Emilie M. Townes, and Angela D. Sims

ACKNOWLEDGMENTS

With one hand on my heart and one on my belly, I offer enormous gratitude to the following beloveds, without whom this book would still be an idea floating around in some other time and space. You, dear ones, have pieces of my heart forever. Thank you.

* * *

Johnny Sears, for being my soul sibling and for believing in this book, in me, and in the women for years now, and for introducing me to the powerful work and people of The Academy for Spiritual Formation. It is because of The Academy that this book, in large part, exists.

My Academy #41 Covenant Group (Cory, Helen, Pam, Lee, Wade, Elizabeth, and Amy), thank you for wanting to read this book long before a word was ever written on the page and for helping me hold hope that Liv would join us on this earth one day. Your interest, accountability, presence, joy, prayer, and steadfast belief helped these women's stories, Liv's story, and my own come to life.

Rev. Becca Stevens and the community of St. Augustine's Chapel, thank you for being a justice-centered and welcoming community to my family and me when we needed a soft place to land, learn, and grow. For your leadership and love, walks and conversations, kindness and care, especially in and through my father's health crisis, I give great thanks.

Rabbi David Horowitz, for being a teacher and a friend and for guiding me through all things midrash as a spiritual practice that can set us free.

Dr. John McClure, for teaching me how to preach from a circle of stories, for treating my idea for this book as precious, sacred, and holy, and for giving me the language of "public witness" for the final section of each chapter.

Ulrike Guthrie, my editor, for your forthright, kind edits that made this book stronger, clearer, and more whole, and to **Chalice Media Group** for thinking that a story about, by, and for women needed to exist in the world.

Mom and Dad, for entrusting me to God, for introducing me to the music and magic of Carole King and Aretha Franklin, and for giving me a pen and paper at such a young age and encouraging me to write, even and especially if all I could write was my own name.

Kent, for being the person I've known the longest on this earth (besides Mom and Dad), for listening to my honesty, for caring about my family and me, and for being my brother and a companion as we heal. Thanks, too, for bringing **Emily** into my life, who brought **Zoe, Clara Jane (CJ),** and **Mathis** into our lives. What gifts you all are.

David and Stephanie, Pat and Tony, thank you for being my family, for checking on me throughout the writing process, and for helping take care of Wade and Liv so I could have extra time to write.

Matthew Eubanks, for always knowing you would one day hold this book in your precious, beautiful hands.

Devon Day Sharp, for being my chosen sister, best friend, godmother to Liv, an early reader of parts of this book, and my attorney. Your eyes, heart, and mind are invaluable, and I am lucky to call you family.

Amy Maureen Skerratt, for being Wade's godmother, a source of strength and joy, my chosen sister, and a firm believer in this book, in women, and in me for years.

Amanda Adams Seitz, for lending your marketing and design skills to the initial proposal that helped this book find a publisher and come to life and for your endless cheerleading, encouragement, and support for me and for the women. Rebecca and Keeley forever.

My grandmothers, Clara Mae and Wanda Lou, I miss you, I love you, and I hope somehow, someway you already know these women's stories as you rest and play in the great beyond.

Anita, my therapist of more than ten years, thank you for your compassionate and perceptive guidance and for inviting me into body, mind, and spirit practices beyond talk therapy. You and your work are a gift.

Marjorie Thompson, my spiritual director, your wisdom and love, kindness and patience, honesty and depth are a healing balm to my healing soul. I will follow you forever.

Drs. Amanda Barrett, Donna Crowe, and Reagan Saig, for saving my life and Liv's, for dedicating your lives to helping women, for helping me heal in those early, painful days when I wasn't sure if I ever would.

Leslie Severns and Ashley Glenn, for being our doulas and for joining the chorus of women who screamed, "Push!" for bearing witness to the trauma and the pain, the strength and the power that is Liv's and my birth story.

Robin Pippin, for strengthening my writing by asking open, honest questions, and for offering your editing and organizational skills to this book in its earliest and most tender stages.

Maria Kane, for your sisterhood, your constant encouragement, your stalwart belief in me, in the women, and in a Gospel of Love, and for your gentle, inquisitive reading of this book that helped deepen my understanding of myself, which made this book a better, truer offering in the world. For a God and a life that would have us meet, write, create, and companion our way through, I give thanks.

Michael Williams, for your presence in the congregation when I preached Eve's story, for your bear-like embrace afterwards, and for telling me that calling her Eve was "brilliant." For being a storyteller and a poet, a mentor and a friend, not only to me but to so many of us on this earth, thank you. I miss you, and I see your smiling face as you commune with the women in the great beyond. It's a beautiful sight to behold. When I see it, I see peace.

Alexandra Lane (and Lisa Yebuah for introducing us), for being the first reader of the women's and my own stories, for sharing your poetic sensibilities, and for being honest when you told me you'd never heard of Anna.

To the women who came before me and to the women who will come after me, your voices are beautiful and necessary, your stories are profound and worth knowing, your lives are precious and worth saving. I will spend the rest of my days working with you for our collective liberation.

To the open plains of West Texas that serve as a portal to a wide-open sky painted by the hands and heart of God, your comfort, your freedom, your love, and your beauty helped raise me; you are a witness to the persistent and ever-present love of God. Thank you for living in my skin, my bones, and my heart forever.

Wade and Liv, you are my whole heart, and you are universes beyond it. You are walking, breathing prayers who gently and sometimes forcefully invite me into deeper healing and growth as a woman, mother, partner, pastor, writer, and friend. For being mine and for being yours and for being each other's, thank you.

Finally, to my beloved, Adam. You're the easiest, even and especially when life is not easy at all. Thank you for being my safest place, and for showing me what love is daily. You've been following women your entire life, and it shows. I love you forever.

Biography

Claire McKeever-Burgett is an author, creative contemplative, and spiritual leader who has dedicated her life to bridging spirituality and social justice. With a background in English and Professional Writing from Baylor University and a Master of Divinity from Vanderbilt Divinity School, she has served as a clergy, led congregations, and facilitated transformative writing, movement, and liturgical practices centered on healing and embodiment. A mother, certified birth and postpartum doula, and a yoga, dance, and martial arts instructor, Claire lives with her family in Nashville, Tennessee. She writes regularly on Substack: *Blessed Are the Women (and other Good News for all of us).*[62]

---

[62] https://clairemckeeverburgett.substack.com/